TOO YOUNG FOR THE TIMES

To: MARK

THANKS FOR YOUR SUPPORT

ENJOY THE BOOK

George Trojan

6-8-2017

CASPER, WY

George V. Trojan

ISBN: 1545485151
ISBN 13: 9781545485156
Library of Congress Control Number: 2017906391
CreateSpace Independent Publishing Platform
North Charleston, South Carolina

PROLOGUE

LWOW, POLAND
September 1, 1939

It's a beautiful summer day, my brother Stefan and I and a few friends were playing soccer on a grass field above the city. We had been at it for an hour plus. Suddenly we heard sirens from the city. As we looked down we did see the German planes turning toward Ulica Lyczakowska - the main East to West connection. Air raid lasted about 45 minutes. When "All Clear" sirens sounded, we were pretty sure that air raid was over and we rushed home.

Mom hugged us both and said that she was worried about us. About the time we got cleaned up, Dad and our brother Henri showed up. Dinner was somewhat subdued; we waited in silence until Mom cleared the table and turned to Dad awaiting his explanation about what we had just witnessed. His mood was somber; he asked what we saw. Stefan and I said that all the aircraft has Swastikas on the tails. Dad said that Hitler had long stated that his foreign policy was based on Lebensraum - aka land expansion for Germany. When you look at map of Europe you will find that to accomplish this he had to move East. Stefan asked if Poland was his target? Dad sat quietly, pondering the question "Yes" he said, "but this is just the beginning."

As we got ready for bed I looked at Stefan. I told him I was scared and hugged him. Little did I know that this day would change my life forever.

Too Young for the Times

Where they came from – no one knew;

Where they were going – no one cared.
Their young bodies grew old with fatigue
And their minds old with fear.
Even HE seemed to have forgotten them.
And yet, they went on –
Strugling, cursing, growing –
Listening only to their souls screaming,
Preserve thyself!
And in despair they asked,
"What for?"

CHAPTER ONE

Saturday, September 2, 1939

Stefan and I slept a little late today; we heard Dad in the living room reading a newspaper and listening to short wave radio for current news. We joined him drinking hot cocoa and eating cookies. He was in good mood. First was a report from Berlin re Polish attack on the radio station in Gleiwitz, Germany. It seems that a group of Polish soldiers attacked the station on Friday night. Germany had no choice but to treat this as a serious incident and a provocation and decided to declare a war with Poland.

Next were messages from England and France advising Germany that they have treaties with Poland and informed Germany that they are in fact in war with Germany. The Chancery Spokesman smugly replied that Germany and Russia have signed a Non-Aggression Treaty early this spring.

Then he chuckled and gave us his crooked smile; it seems that he found a source on the radio that had a different take on the attack on the Radio Station, it seems that attacking soldiers were in fact German Prisoners. WOW!

For Poland, it was a tough situation; Germans coming from the West and the Russians from the East – not a good situation to be in.

The Family took a leisurely walk around Kaiserwald Hills overlooking the city. It seemed so peaceful, and yet, we knew that it will change in not too distant future.

By dinner time Dad had lost his good humor; when Mom called for dinner, he went to the kitchen and filled his brandy glass. His face was somber now – he brought a piece of paper and pencil with him. He smiled with tears in his eyes – he wrote something on the piece of paper; took a sip of is brandy – picked up the piece of paper, looked at it and whispered through his tears – "WWII is here".

CHAPTER TWO

Russian Occupation

September encouraging a Government in Exile kin England. Dad looked at us and spoke slowly, "the end is near, may God have mercy on us". On September 21ˢᵗ Poland surrendered.

Russian and Forces met in Lwow. There were negotiations between Germans and Russians for couple of days. Finally, German Forces retired to the West. Polish Brigadier General Langner signed Surrender Protocol on September 22ⁿᵈ. Terms of surrender called for a free passage of defenders of the city to Hungary and Romania. Russians did not honor Agreement and arrested 2000 Officers 800 Members of the Cabinet. They were transported to Tarnopol, POW Camp on the border with Russia. As the word spread that Russians were pouring Dad, Stefan and I went down to Lyczakowska ulica to watch the arrival of the Russian Army. It was quite a sight. They were the dirties and wildest people I have ever seen. The street was full of them – just marching forward – occasionally bending down and picking up a piece of military equipment left behind by our soldiers. I nearly burst with laughter when I saw of them pour to-bacco into newspaper, roll it and then smoke it.

Their uniforms and equipment were pathetic. Instead of packs, they carried cotton bags tied to them by rope – the blankets were carried in a roll over the right or the left shoulder. Their rifles looked old – (later I found out that they were manufactured in 1903) – and they had extremely long bayonets affixed to the bar-rel. Even to me, they looked grim, and yet somehow pathetic.

The soldiers just plowed on straight ahead, without any noise; once in a while bending down over equipment surrendered by the Polish Army which piled high on the grass plots along the side walk. They would exchange their equipment with ours without so much as stopping. The middle of the boulevard was crowded with tanks and trucks. Buses were decorated with pictures of Stalin and Lenin and various other heroes of the Russian Revolution, this stream of humanity and equipment continued for about 3 days and nights. We left early, had enough of it.

Mom was waiting for us; her eyes full of concern. Dad went into the kitchen and poured himself a glass of brandy, returned to living room and sat in his favorite chair. He asked Stefan of his opinion of what we saw.

He pondered this question, looked around and aid quietly, "we are in for a very hard future". Dad nodded, and then added softly, "we must keep a very low profile for a while". Sleep was tough, full of terrible dreams.

Slowly things returned to normal. We were becoming accus-tomed to seeing Russians everywhere. Soon a new phrase was added to our vocabulary – NKVD – "Niewiesz Kiedy Wrocisz do Domu" translated into Polish it means – "Never know when you re-turn home" – it was ironic, but true. For this was the abbreviation for the dreaded secret Police.

As the front-line troops moved on, their place was taken by troops seasoned in handling civilian population, plus large con-tingents of NKVD. Daily, new orders and regulations were being proclaimed. First, the city of Lwow and the entire region of Galicia was proclaimed to be part of the Russian Republic it was to be known as Ukrainian Socialistic Republic. Secondly, National language was now Russian or Ukrainian. Polish was not to be used. Three, every citizen of Ukrainian Republic must register and apply for passport as soon as possible; they had 2 categories – 2 years and 6 months; the latter was scary. The City was full of Refugees who really created drain on the economy. By October, NKVD went into action against Refugees for illegal passports. In December alone 2000 plus were arrested and sent to Labor Camps in Russia.

We used to out every Sunday for a walk around the town; have a nice lunch on sidewalk Café/Restaurant and enjoy the scenery. All this was gone. The beautiful Cosmopolitan town was trashed. As we continued home, I could see that Mom was in tears. Dad held her closer and whispered something to her. She shook her head and smiled. She was happy to have us all together.

After drinking tea and having few cookies, Dad went to living room to listen to his shortwave radio. He felt that would be banned shortly. Polish Newspapers were already shut down. Next day new proclamation; word "Sir" is not to be used; it is being replaced by comrade". Later that day another announcement Polish currency "zloty" is being phased out. You were urged to take all Polish currency to the nearest Bank and exchange it for Rubles. The exchange rate was one Ruble equals 10 Zlotys. Another blow to the economy. Dad just shook his head and said, "where did we go wrong to deserve this fate.

CHAPTER THREE

Russian Occupation
Fall 1939

Soon our free days were over. The proclamation announced that schools were to open and everyone of school age had to register – compulsory education. Where we had ten years of secondary schooling, the Russian system had twelve, and so everyone past third grade was moved back two years. I anxiously awaited the return to school. I had grown tired of the vacation and was eager to meet new friends and join the school fun. The really wasn't too much difference in the system. We still went to school six days a week; now, however, we had to take Russian language. Religion was dropped and there was no more praying before and after the classes. It soon became monotonous, since we didn't have any text books. All teachers were dictating from the only hand book provided to them by the regime. I spent hours writing and taking notes. But we managed to go on, and in a way, we managed to enjoy it. One thing became obvious immediately. In everything we studied, the Russian Revolution and its heroes were glorified. It became ridiculous, especially in mathematics. All written problems dealt with the Red Army or some other division of the regime. Being as young as we were, we offered some resistance to this regimentation. I remember distinctly one occasion – our Russian teacher was a young woman who apparently was married to one of the officers in the Red Army. She really was very pleasant and we liked very much. On this occasion, due to a mix-up, she was scheduled or first class. As she walked into the class room, she turned white. On the blackboard was drawn a large cross. The whole class stood up while a member recited aloud the "Our Father". After the prayer, we sat down and awaited her reaction. Visibly shaken, she asked us in a pleading voice not to ever do this again. The last portion of the class was devoted to reading; she was just too upset to conduct any lecture.

The Government was getting organized and new proclamations were being issued daily. The latest one had changed the week from seven days to six; work five and rest on the sixth. This was an obvious to curb the activities of the church. Of course, local churches reacted by having Masses scheduled at many odd hours to permit those who were working to attend.

Next, property owners were evicted from their properties which were taken over by the State. We heard people say that soon all private properties would be taken over by the State; this of course would include the peasants; who would then belong to a kolhoz. The latter we didn't mind, as a lot of resentment was building up against the profit they were making of human misery. Slowly but surely, one item after another became plentiful and we could eat once again without worrying what we were going to for the next day.

Clothing and shoes and any other necessities of this type were still difficult to get, and when the rumor started that certain store would sell on the following day, the people would line up the previous evening in order to be one of the first to get in and make a purchase. These long vigils were sometimes interrupted by the Police would drive up in the trucks, load everyone on, and drive approximately ten miles out. Then they would let everyone out of the trucks and make them walk back home. The regime was trying to discourage signs of inadequate supply of goods.

CHAPTER FOUR

Russian Occupation
Fall 1939

As the months passed, the weather changed into steady rain and mud. It was getting cold, and the days were getting shorter and shorter. The weather did stop the Regime from issuing new proclamations; the latest one really hit home. We finally learned about the 6 month passports issued to property owners. Under the Constitution, private ownership of property was forbidden; thus, all property owners were required to give up the ownership of properties and resettle. The term – "enemy of the State" was being heard more and more. The NKVD became well known for their arrests of political prisoners. Rumors kept persisting about existence of a "Black List" containing names of people who were to be resettled to Siberia for crimes against the State. Nobody felt safe. Informers were turning up everywhere, and who could what stories had been relayed to the NKVD? Children in school were encouraged to talk about their parents and their activities. The promise of a reward was even mentioned for anyone turning in undesirable citizens. Even priests had quieted down their sermons during the services.

Then it did happen – in the middle of the night. NKVD trucks came speeding through the night in October, rounding up persons on the "black list". It was always the same. In the middle of the night came a loud knock on the door. "Are you Mr. and Mrs. So, and so'? You have been charged with crimes against the State. You have 15 minutes to pack. You are allowed to carry one suitcase and a hand bag. Everything else must be left behind for the family of some Russian Officer.

Nobody was given the opportunity to explain. The order was final. The only thing left was to pack and face the new disaster. In most cases, families were split up, with husband going one way and the wife another. In cases where the family had small children, they became the property of the State to be turned over to some organization to be brought up as young communists, ignorant of their parents. No one will ever know how many people were deported in the few weeks that followed. The destination was always Siberia or some distant Republic where the labor was needed to cultivate the land or work in the mines.

Most of the families of Polish intelligentsia were evacuated. Priests and former Police officers also were taken away, and thousands of others, by virtue of their association with former regime, victims of paid informers, were sent on their way. Mother was s visibly shaken by all this. She was Afraid, I suppose that should any one of us say the wrong thing, the word would spread, and possibly someone else, an informer, then might find out. Then soon, we too would have to leave. But we carried on and the nights passed uneventfully. We had some close calls, like some neighbors in the same building were evacuated and we all felt that our time had come.

The plight of the poor deportees was beyond description. The weather was very cold by the time these deportations were initiated. The deportees were herded into box cars which were left standing on the siding for several days, without any food or heat.

Many died of starvation and exposure even before leaving the city. People, friends and relatives, crowding the railroad station were kept away from the trains by the Police. They could only watch helplessly and be witness to what was happening. I don't think I will ever forget the sight of dead bodies being thrown out of the cars into the snow, later to be picked up by trucks and dumped into unmarked graves. And still, there was no let up. The round up continued. Always at night – always the knock on the door, the reading of charges and the brief order to get ready. The desired effect, if such was, has been accomplished. E very one was afraid; no one trusted anyone. Even in the school things changed. We no longer mentioned the war or talked about hidden sabers, carbines, or any other piece of material for war.

Our circle of friends grew steadily smaller. To our inquiries as to the whereabouts of certain people, Mother would answer vaguely that they had Probably gone to visit some friends. The strain on her had begun to show. Her hair turned gray and she no longer sang while cooking. When we came home, we were welcomed as though we had been gone for a long time. Stefán too, had changed. He had grown more serious and really acted as a big brother. He always saw to it that we were together, and even chose the people with whom we associated.

Some of the friends we both knew joined the Pionier organization in school. They seemed to a lot of fun, always doing something or going somewhere. I didn't particularly care a bout wearing the red scarf, and anyway, Mother and Stefan would always give an emphatic "no" to my inquiries about joining the group. Mother would always say that the war was not over; that no one knew what the future had in store for us. Then she would point to the mass evacuation of our friends because of some informer's stories. Do you want this happen to us? Do you want someone to call you "Communist?". This I could not understand. Why should I become communist just by joining the Pioniers? But, their will prevailed and I didn't join.

CHAPTER FIVE

Russian Occupation
Winter Months 1939

The months passed on and soon it was Christmas. God, how different it was this time! There was none of the anxious anticipation, no thought of gifts or even the food of the Season. Usually Mom started cooking and baking weeks ahead to feed a large crowd, for the entire family gathered t our home for this occasion. This time there was no baking except for couple of cakes and some b read. There was traditional fish prepared in Jewish style, and that was it. I think that it was most depressing Christmas I have ever known.

Soon, it was back to school. Since I wasn't allowed to join the Pioniers I joined an altar boy club at the Franciscan Monastery. It really was a lot of fun. The priests were young men and very kind. It wasn't too long before I learned my Latin and was able to serve t the altar. This seemed to please Mom too. I had a nice group of friends and priests always managed to have something to occupy us – be it a play or some other useful project. It was really a very pleasant association. The priests were simply wonderful friends. They joined us frequently in playing soccer or volleyball. At first, it was rather odd to see priest chasing soccer ball, his cassock just flying in the breeze. But as the days progressed, I realized that they too were human beings with conventional likes and dislikes.

Fathers Leon and Roch, and Father Kozak, our Director, were particularly close to us. Besides playing, we had various study groups, dealing primarily with literature and writing. Each Sunday we would meet, and discuss some play or a book. Some would write short stories or compositions and would read them aloud, and later we would all join in constructive criticism. The priests were really very easy to get along with. They seemed to have endless patience and understanding. It was as though they realized that there was a war going on and that we needed some love and affection.

I used to enjoy serving High Mass for Father Roch. He had an excellent voice; and the Latin always sounded very beautiful when he sang. I remember the first time I ever served Mass for him – when it came time for the offering, I brought the wine and the water to the altar. I just kept pouring the wine into the chalice and almost emptied the cruet. I was so afraid that there wouldn't be enough left for the second offering that I went back into sacristy and brought back more wine. After the Mass, I was given a lecture by Father Roch about this. Finally, he said with a smile, "what would parishioners say if they knew that I had double shot during the Mass?". I got the hint, and have never again increased the portion.

The Monastery was very beautiful and very old. The surrounding grounds were picturesque and inviting. The garden was large; it was surrounded by a high wall, full of apple trees and flowers. There was a wide walk carved in the green grass; it went straight back to the wall, and then curved left and right and followed the wall. Along the wall were figures of various saints. Here the priests and the brothers took their walks at night and said their prayers.

It was very peaceful here. Although we were not allowed to play in the garden, we could visit there with our friends. It was very relaxing to walk along the path with a priest, asking the multitude of questions about anything that came to mind of a young boy.

In the winter time, I used to serve at the early Mass and then go to school from the church. I enjoyed the walk from the street car stop, watching the city as it awoke. One by one windows would be illuminated by glowing lights as the occupants of the houses awoke and got ready for the daily toils. The snow too felt nice and clean. I felt as though I was going through some unknown land, making fresh tracks for a new civilization.

The early Mass was very popular and the Church was generally crowded. One day as I approached the Church through the side door, Brother Henry motioned to me and asked if I would mind serving the Mass in the back Chapel. "No, it will be alright," I replied. This was something new for me. I knew that there was a Chapel behind the main altar, separated from it by a wall, but I never knew that anyone ever celebrated a Mass there. Since I was late, I didn't get a chance to say anything before the door opened, and I was pushed in. Slowly, I advanced toward the altar. Everything was so quiet and so dark. I took my position along the altar and recited the Latin with the priest. Finally, came the time for Holy communion. As I look back, I know I almost cried out in fright. For from every corner of the room, there approached what seemed a mob of dark figures. Their heads were covered with hoods, and over their clasped hands they wore the cord sash which is worn around their hips and usually hangs on the left side. This was indeed an eerie assembly. Slowly, I realized who they were. These were the Brothers accepting their daily Holly Communion. I almost laughed aloud as the relief seemed to weaken my limbs. When I got to school, I related my encounter with the monks to my friends, who shared with my laughter. I can't remember now what went through my mind at the sight of these dark and silent figures, but I do know that the shadows didn't help any.

CHAPTER SIX

Russian Occupation
Winter Months of 1940

On my way to the school I had to pass by a kaserne presently occupied by Red Army units. Each morning I would meet the troops just as they were coming through the gate, stripped to the waist, trotting in columns of four. It was quite a sight. This was apparently their exercise period, for they would run up the streets for couple of miles and then return to the kaserne. On the return trip, they marched and sang. This always struck me as a very picturesque experience. They really sand beautifully. One man would sing the verse, and then the entire group would join with the refrain. As I watched them, I asked myself: "How could I possibly hate them?". They seemed to be such nice people. Really, alone they quite simple and good people.

I remember what I then considered a friendship with a Russian boy, Vania, whose father was a Red Army Officer. He was nice enough and often I would go to his house to eat, he would come to our house. We never discussed anything of importance; but yet, the friendship seemed to be there, and I think, had we met under different circumstances, we could have really become good friends. One time, as I sat to dinner with him, his father came in. He introduced me, and his father immediately began questioning me. Nothing of any importance, but yet, the questions kept coming. He seemed to be very interested in our lives before the war; the politics, the opportunities for the young people; but somehow, I just could not open up. I was afraid, I suppose. I answered in generalities, wondering when he would grow angry with me and stop asking those questions. Finally, he stopped and we sat down to eat. Just as I was ready to sit up from the table, he spoke again. "Do you really believe in God," he asked? The question caught me by surprise. "Of course, I do," came my short reply. "Have you ever seen him?", he retorted. "No, I did not; but it doesn't matter. This is unexplainable; this is faith." At this laughed jovially and the cordiality was restored. Vania and I were permitted to retire to the other room for a game of chess.

On the way home that night I kept thinking about my encounter with Vania's father. Would something be said to him after my departure? Would I be able visit him again? Somehow, I hoped that nothing would happen to endanger our friendship. I was amazed with myself how cautious I had grown in the past few months. Was he really interested in our past lives or was it just a smart ruse? I thought it best not to take such a chance again and vowed not to get involved in such discussions in the future. This was a vow which I did not break for many years.

Now that the snow had melted and the ground become dry once more, the action against the partisans had begun once again. Each day we read in the paper where more skirmishes were held and more people were killed or taken prisoners. By now, however, the bands were larger; apparently, during the long winter season, the partisans had actively engaged in recruiting. Many young people ran away into the woods to hide, and once there, joined the partisans for a variety of reasons.

At home too, things have somehow changed. Mom and Dad kept to themselves; Dad rarely discussed politics at home; that was a big change. He still would have his brandy after dinner and retire to bed early. Our sister Ann visited on either Saturday or Sunday; Her husband and 2 little girls would come along. Mom was always glad to see them; this was her chance to spoil her granddaughters; Everything should have been normal, but yet it wasn't. Something was going on that was creating some anxiety and tension. I could not put my finger on it, though I tried. I even mentioned it to Stefan but he only laughed and accused me of having wild imagination.

CHAPTER SEVEN

Russian Occupation
Spring – Summer 1941

That Sunday, as usual, Ann, John and the children came over for dinner. John was really wonderful. An electrical engineer by trade, he had taught himself a lot about basic electricity. We sat through many hours listening to his discussions about various electrical applications. Radio was his specialty, and he was employed by a radio station before the war as chief engineer. He was a pleasant fellow, rather tall and with dark complexion, and his once jet black hair was thinning at the top and on the sides. Always quick with a smile, he was very gentle with his children.

He too was a member of the Polish Army, and when the campaign began, he was sent over to Warsaw to defend it. Fortunately, in a sense, he was disarmed by the Germans and was soon released to go home. He returned approximately six weeks after the capitulation. However, he could not forget the war and the NAZI onslaught. He hated Germans with passion and often declared that he was glad and thanked God, since we had to occupied, that we were under Russians and not the Germans. He was very nationalistic in his feelings and, I suppose, could never forgive the Germans for attacking as they did.

As we ate the dinner, he carelessly mentioned that he had a telephone call from Janusz (his former Commander), during the week, and that the latter wanted to be remembered to us. Eagerly, we asked him about news of his activities. But he only smiled and replied; "Now, you all are old enough to know that such things are never discussed over the telephone." Then he added that Janusz was well and that things were really going well for him. He had under his command a small group of terrorists who would soon be known to us as "Liberators". We were all happy that young friend could survive the winter and that he was doing so well. Only Mother uttered concern over his activities, saying that young people these days should not be hot-headed. She felt that things would work out for themselves and that we should not be so eager to create more trouble. John laughed and said, "Mother, you are just worried about your little children". It was a pleasant day, and being in a generally happy frame of mind, we all took a walk in the park.

By now summer has passed and the winter was again approaching rapidly. Our friend Janusz kept his promise. The acts of terrorism against the regime were increasing rapidly. No longer did you see Ukrainian Policeman on the beat alone; they travelled in pairs. No one was safe from the underground, and the informers especially paid the highest penalty.

It was common knowledge that the underground set up a court to handle complaints against fellow citizens. The informer would be tried in absentia. If his guilt was sufficiently established, an assassination team would knock on the door, force their way in, read the verdict and then shoot the victim with silenced pistols. The verdict signed by the court would be left on the body. The court showed no mercy, and its verdicts were speedily executed.

Soon more proclamations were issued by the regime. Anyone apprehended and found to be in possession of firearms or ammunition, or anything that could be construed as a dangerous

weapon, would be sentenced to death. Anyone harboring a criminal, or having any knowledge of the whereabouts of members of
the resistance group and not disclosing this to the authorities,
would also be punished by death. The war was on.

One afternoon after coming home from school, I noticed that
Mother had company. Ann was with her and they both have been
crying. Anxiously I inquired what was wrong? Mother just hugged
me and said, "John is joining up". Janusz needs a good communication man and John agreed to join him. Crazy! What does he think
he can do? Win the war single-handed? He has family to support
and he cannot and should not do this to them. He has no right.
What could I say, just barely thirteen years of age? Should I argue
the point with them and prove to them that there was more at
stake than just our everyday lives? There were far more important
things to think about than our immediate families. No, I couldn't
even understand those things myself. It was wonderful for someone else to do these things, but these members of my own family
endangering themselves and their loved ones. No, this was out of
the question. He must be stopped before it is too late.

Later, that evening John came over to discuss the situation.
We all set around the table in the living room as we had done on
many occasions in the past. Slowly and deliberately he began his
speech. "You all have the right to know my decision and why it had
to be made. We are all members of one family, dependent upon
one another. In normal times, situations like this would not arise.
But these are not normal times, and sacrifices are required. I have
watched my men die at the front, helpless against the steel mon-
sters of the German Panzer Armies. Yet, they did not give up until
they were sold out by our own government. They kept on fighting,
believing that what they were doing was necessary, regardless of
price. Many good men died in those short 29 days; I cannot bring
myself to forget and let believing that what they were doing was
necessary, regardless of price. Many good men died in those short

29 days; I cannot bring myself to forget them and to let them die in vain. I must continue doing my part. I am a Pole and proud of it; I am proud of my heritage.

I know the objections. I'm family man and my family should come first. His voice quiet now, full of passionate expression for the belief that he professed. For him, there was no alternative. "Besides", he continued, "I am not going to leave home. I will continue to maintain my job at the radio station. The only thing that the organization has asked of me that I train other men in radio transmission and repair. Meantime, I must maintain secret radio contact with our government in London. The radio station will be moved frequently to escape detection; it will not be located in our building. This should not endanger Ann and the children too much. The broadcasts will be few and they will be short in duration. The school will take a lot of my time, but this cannot be helped. Now, I have said all I'm going to say, except that I'm placing myself in your hands. Whether we like it or not, we are in it now. With God's help, we will see it through to better times. Then he fell silent, and slowly looked at each of us. When he came to me, his voice softened.

"Son, this is a hell of way to grow up. Remember, you are a man now. You have the same responsibilities as we, the older people. you must be very careful of what you say to your friends. I noticed a certain look of pride in your eyes. Perhaps I should be flattered, but I'm not. Pride brings on bragging, and the need to discuss the events with others. Get rid of it". His voice was hard and his eyes were looking straight at me. "I'm not a hero," he continued, "I'm but a man who believes that as long a man has two arms and legs and can think, his life belongs to his country, especially in these dark days, when so many of our people have turned against us". Again, he fell silent.

This time Stefan spoke up, his voice quivering as he started. "Since this seems to be night for confessions, I too must make an admission. John, I am glad for you, and I hope that many others will follow you. We should all wake up and realize that the struggle has never stopped; it merely changed its style. Soldiers no longer fight in trenches. Now they wear civilian clothes and fight dirty". Here he stopped, turned to Mother, took her hand gently and continued. "Perhaps you will condemn me for this, Mother, but I too have joined the movement. My contribution is very small; all younger people act as couriers between the groups. I never know anyone nor do I see anyone. I just go to prearranged place and either pick up or deliver a message, as the case may be. It is very insignificant, and it has been working for us. The Russians never suspect anything. You are probably wondering where a boy my age could meet the proper people. Well, our old friend Janusz consented to this after much persuasion. We now have well over thirty boys acting as messengers." This, of course, was very shattering news; nobody even dreamed of anything like this. Anxiously I watched Mother. She was taken aback by this confession. Her eyes revealed her concern and sadness. Silently, she took Stefan's hand and pressed it to her mouth. Then she embraced him gently, rocking him as she did when he was still her little boy. "No, my son, I guess I cannot blame you anymore than I could blame John. This is a crazy world we are living in these days and I suppose you all just grow up to fast. You are men before you boys. I just hope that I will not fail you when you need me".

The discussion ended. We all agreed that as individuals we had no control over our destinies; that only time would tell where or when we would meet our Maker. I shall always remember that long night, for this was when I first realized that Stefan and I would no longer be together. He had grown past me, and circumstances were calling on him to do things other than just play. And the following days were sad indeed. It was a long time before I could adjust to that fact. Stefan was home less and less, and when he did get home he was dead tired both physically and mentally. We no longer shed mutual interests and I felt sad and lonely, angry that the fate had made me too young for the times. When I complained, Stefan would laugh and say, "Boy, before this thing is over, you are going to wish that you were little boy again." God, how prophetic these words proved to be in the years that followed.

CHAPTER EIGHT

Russian Occupation
Fall and Winter 1941

The activities of John and Stefan made me now more than ever aware that underground was really intensifying its reign of terror against the regime with each passing day. The assassinations of Ukrainian policemen were now an almost daily routine; destruction of railroad tracks and other lines of communication were a daily occurrence. Soon it was wintertime again, and another Christmas rolled around. This time the gathering at our house included Janusz. This was only our second meeting, but I noticed that he was much happier this time. Apparently, he was enjoying his role as a resistance leader, engaged in the struggle with the government. He still looked very youthful, although his eyes and mouth had never lost their sternness. He was serious at the table, and never discussed the work he was doing other than to make a general comment about John's and Stefan's making valuable contributions to the movement. He thanked Mother and Ann for being understanding, and b egged their forgiveness for the necessity of it, but he never expressed regret at having inspired both to join the movement.

The meal was over quickly and Janusz rose to say goodbye. As he was leaving, he walked around the table to Mother, took her hands in his and said, "thank you very much for a wonderful meal and company. Then he placed his lips on Mother's forehead, and without another word, he was gone. We stayed up a little longer, but no one seemed to be in the mood for discussions. We decided to go to bed early and get some rest. Once in bed, I could not go to sleep. So much had happened in the past two months, and now both John and Stefan were deeply involved in the covert activities against the present government. I could not help but wonder what would happen to me and Mother, and of course, Anna and the children, should one of them get caught. Was John right in is argument that night? Did he really have the right to sacrifice everything to satisfy his conscience? How would he feel if someone were to divulge to the authorities that he was a member of the underground and we would be arrested because of it? I grew increasingly confused and scared. I didn't want to be separated from the rest of family; I could not visualize life without them. My God, when will all this end, and when will we able to return to the normal life that decent people deserve?

CHAPTER NINE

Russian Occupation
Spring and Summer 1942

The weeks to come were extremely difficult and sad. Dad was bed ridden upstairs from lung problems, so it was Mother and I were alone. John and Stefan were always gone. We missed Janusz very; we had grown to love him like a member of the family. Mother worried about him, wondering if he had grown strong enough to return to is work. Finally, John noticed how unhappy we were, and he decided that it would be a good idea I he, Ann and the children moved back in with us. We all welcomed the idea. It would be nice to have full house again, and perhaps the grandchildren would occupy Mother so she wouldn't worry. Slowly things returned to normal. No one ever mentioned Janusz anymore. Springtime came and passed unnoticed as slowly the summer approached. I looked forward to a long vacation. It will be nice to get out and play in the hills, I thought. Summer was so nice; so many things to do; soccer, swimming, and at night, play hide and seek.

And then it happened. Germany declared war on Russians. I listened to it in disbelief. The two partners, who together had portioned Poland were now fighting each other. How was it possible? What had happened and why did Hitler decide to end the partnership? These questions were running through my mind as I looked over the newspaper. The article described how the German Forces struck without warning, crossing the bridge over river San at Przemysl. The door opened and Stefan and John walked in. Stefan was extremely happy but John was serious, almost angry. Stefan laughingly said to me that we would shortly have new liberators. Then, turning to Mother, he added; "John isn't happy over the news. I guess he hates the Germans worse than the Russians. I really don't care; I hate them both; I only hope that they destroy each other, thus making our job of rescuing Poland from them both that much easier." John didn't even reply.

The news about the German attack spread like a wildfire. It was received with mixed feelings. Some were glad to see them tangle with the Russians, while others just glad to see Russians go, for nobody doubted that the Germans would destroy the Russians. Of course, there were those who had cooperated with the regime and now had no choice but to leave and cast their lot with it. For these I had no pity. They would be paid for their greed. The chaos associated with the hostilities returned once more. The streets were jammed with trucks filled to the brim with goods that the Russians were liquidating and taking home with t hem. They were caught by complete surprise, and everyone knew there would be no of Lwow.; the city would be abandoned without a fight. That in itself was good news.

For approximately three days or more the Lyczakowski Boulevard was clogged with military and civilian traffic. Everyone was moving East toward Russia. Stefan and I used to go and watch chaos. We were happy; and though we had grown to hate Russians, I thought about Vania and wondered what would happen to him. He was a nice boy, although he was Russian and a Communist. I guess he could not help it; he was brought up. New terror now grasped the city; The NKVD, the Russian Secret Police, started rounding up known suspects and summarily executing them, while underground openly attacked convoys at night. No one was safe anymore. The nights were why would shattered by gunfire. A quick burst of machine gun fire would greet a lone truck moving down the street. Everyone found that riding in a Russian truck was declared an enemy, else why would they be leaving with them? And so, the slaughter went on. No one ever knew when the day would turn into a nightmare.

Meanwhile, the opposition to the advancing German Forces was crumbling. In a very short time, the advancing contingent of the German Army was within artillery range of the city. The city itself lay in the valley, surrounded by hills. The western end of the city held a commanding view towards the east, and the German artillerymen were taking every advantage of the situation. Every time a vehicle appeared on top of Lyczakowski Blvd., it was spotted by the German observers, and shortly one could hear the whistle of approaching artillery shells. We had an excellent view of this from our balcony.

As the German drew nearer, the exodus the of the main from the city increased in proportion. Everything that could provide transportation was being utilized. And every few minutes, the Germans would shell the top of the main boulevard. The people would panic, but just went on, hoping that shells would miss them. All were not that fortunate. The entire area was filled with dead bodies and carcasses of dead animals. The remains of the truck destroyed by the shellfire were pushed aside by the tanks, and the steam of humanity at night, the spectacle was particularly awesome. To the west, the sky would light up as though some giant searchlights were sweeping the skies, followed by the whistle of shells. The German artillery was at work again. This went on for three days and nights. To add to the horror for the evacuees, the Germans started using aircraft to stop the exodus.

I remember one particular afternoon. Stefan and I were standing on the sidewalk, surveying the situation. We looked at the blank stares of the civilians sitting atop crowded trucks, their faces expressionless. They were scared and confused, afraid of what the future held in the store for them. Their good living had come to an abrupt end and now they were living from day to day, hopping to escape from the Germans and settle down somewhere to live out the war. As we stood there watching the grim parade, we heard some singing. In disbelief, we turned and saw a group of young Konsomols, marching and singing. "Jak shczo zaftra woyna, kaksdzo zafta pochod, za swobodnoju rodinu postaniem kak odyn czeloviek, sovietskiej narod za svobodnoju roddynu postaniem" --- "If the war should come tomorrow, we shall march tomorrow. WE shall rise; the entire Soviet Nation would rise in defense of our soil." How ironic we thought.

There they were singing a military song about defending their country, and yet they were abandoning this city, with no hope of stemming the tide. What were they trying to prove? Were they trying to prove to themselves that their faith in the Communist system remained unshaken? I glanced at Stefan, who visibly enjoying this grotesque scene. His face was twisted with hate, and through clenched teeth I heard him say. "Sing you sons of bitches. You won't live long enough to defend your God-damned country." Again, I realized how much older he really was then I, while I hated them, I felt sorry for them. To me they were still human beings, confused, lost, but never the less, human beings. To him, they represented everything he hated and he had not an ounce of pity for them. As far as he was concerned, they deserved everything they were getting, and more.

Suddenly, we heard some shouting. As we turned toward the noise, we heard Russian soldier scream; "Germansy samoloty" – German aircraft." We looked up and saw approximately 25 Heinkel 111, German bombers. They were flying in perfect formation about 2000 feet, headed in our direction. Before I had a chance to say anything, Stefan grabbed me and shouted at me to follow him he took off on dead run, away from the boulevard. I followed him in close pursuit. Behind us we could hear the shooting increasing in the intensity, and the noise of the aircraft engines getting louder and louder. I glanced over my shoulder, and that the aircraft were almost over our heads. Then something silver dropped from the lead aircraft. "Stefan, they are dropping the bombs," I screamed in fright. To confirm this, we could hear the whistle of falling bombs. By this time, we were some distance away from the boulevard. We hit the ground and prayed that the bombs would miss us. The noise of exploding bombs was deafening. Now, they were exploding all around us, and we could see ricks flying in the air, as houses were being hit. The street below us was a ghostly spectacle. Burning trucks and dead horses were everywhere. People were trying to escape the holocaust on foot, above them.

The constant noise of the aircrafts, as wave after wave flew over to dump its cargo of destruction. I don't know how long it lasted, but it seemed like an eternity. We saw a couple of plains receive direct hits. As flames enveloped them, we would see the crews parachuting out. They didn't have a chance. Everyone who had a weapon was shooting at them. We saw coyle of flyers falling through the air, their burning parachutes trailing behind them, completely useless. Then the aircraft were gone. We had no desire to return to the boulevard. We just ran home.

That afternoon, accompanied by John, we went to investigate the damage caused by the air raid. It was beyond description. There were dead bodies all over the place; some were charred beyond recognition, others just bloody and silent. Burning vehicles were being cleared from the road to permit the traffic to continue. The dead bodies were just being dumped on the grass plots around the sidewalk to be cared for by somebody else. We continued our walk toward the church of St. Mary of Ostrobramski. Here, the boulevard was at its highest elevation and here was the greatest damage. We counted 15 craters, approximately 15 feet apart., all direct hits on the boulevard. There were ss me patterns a few yards to the left and to the right. Here, the dead bodies were stacked five feet high. The stench was unbearable. On our left, the Lychakowski Railroad Station was burning, the result of several direct hits. Railroad cars were burning in the yard, with dead bodies scattered all round. I could stand it no longer; I felt sick at my stomach, and soon had to step aside and vomit. John took pity on me. "let's go home," he said curtly to Stefan. I have never been able to forget that day. This was war at its worst moment. That night I asked John why the civilian population was allowed to suffer so much since they had no direct part in the war. He merely shrugged his shoulders and said, "During the last war they said it was bad. Now we say it's bad, who knows what the people who will follow us will say when they have their war?"

The siege continued for the next three days. Always in our ears the whistle of falling bombs and the shrieking of frightened humans and animals, and in our eyes the ever-present sight of death. At night, the flashes of the artillery batteries firing on their taets, and invariably, the loud whistling noise, like a truck rounding a sharp curve too fast, followed by the explosion on impact. We grew accustomed to these sounds, and even stopped going into the cellar at night. Then by Saturday, things quieted down. John was now really tense. He stayed close to home, since his radio station inoperative. The underground too was anxious., not knowing what to expect, but stubbornly attacking lonely tucks trying to make it out of town. The entire tet us? Situation seemed so confusing with no one what to expect. Some were happy to see the Russians go, but they could not help wondering what the future would bring. How would the Germans treat us? By this time, we had become weary of "Liberators".

CHAPTER TEN

German Occupation
Summer 1942

Sunday was very beautiful and quiet. The sun was shining brightly and the weather promised to be warm and relaxing. I couldn't explain it, but something was hanging in the air and I felt a sense of anxiety and anticipation. And then it came. A neighbor rushed into our house shouting, "The Germans are here." We immediately rushed to the boulevard below, hoping to see for ourselves. Yes, it was true. It was approximately 10 am, and the sidewalks were lined up with happy people, waving flowers and shouting greetings. I too felt happy. These soldiers looked much better than anything I had ever seen before.

First came the motorcycles with sidecars, on which were mounted machineguns; recon elements I supposed. They went by at a pace, racing up the boulevard. A few minutes several scout cars followed also at rather fast pace everyone going east, following the retreating Russians, trying to determine where they were. Then, slowly, came the main body. First came the infantry. They seemed so happy and so young. They were walking in single file on each side of the street, their shirt sleeves rolled up, smiling, impressed with the happy welcome they were receiving from the civilians. Down the middle of the road came the motorized elements. I had never seen so many vehicles. Then came the large half-tracts, filled with soldiers, smiling and waving with both hands to the people on the sidewalks, towing behind them the artillery pieces we had to know so swell.

The soldiers stopped occasionally to hand out bits of chocolate and cookies to the children. Thank God, they were very different. I felt much better now. I had gained faith in these happy people. I could not believe that they could or would do us any harm. The march continued, and again came the infantry, marching and singing. This time the words were unfamiliar, but, the melody was very beautiful. They sang in three voices, and it sounded very impressive. Stefan and I walked down the boulevard enjoying the scenery. This was really something, we thought. We were greatly impressed with the modern equipment of the German Army. We walked eastward, and as we approached the church of St. Mary Ostrobramski, we noticed that the bells were tolling. Soon other bells began to ring and we felt like shouting with joy. It was a good feeling. We felt as though the war was already over and things had returned to normal. We were happy in anticipation.

The crowds on the sidewalk continued to increase, everyone so happy, waving flowers at the troops. The small children, bewildered by all this, just looked anfd smiled as the soldiers stopped and patted them on the head, or pinched their little cheeks. Yes, these were good people; I was convinced. Right across the street from the church was a park, and we noticed that some units were pulling off the road and parking their vehicles in the shade of the shade of the trees. Curious, we went over to see what they were doing. I suppose that to them it was normal routine to their vehicles, pitch their little tents, and take care of their equipment.

As we continued down the gravel walkway, we came upon a small group of Germans sitting in front of their tents, their vehicles s parked nearby. They were young and seemed carefree. As we approached, we noticed that one of them had an accordion. We stopped and waited for the show. Soon a happy filled the air and we heard the soldiers join in singing. This seemed so remote from the activity all around us, that we couldn't help but just stand there and watch. Soon we were noticed by a young soldier who motioned for us to come over. Eagerly we joined him. He spoke very pleasantly to us, but unfortunately, we could not understand him. We just stood there and grinned and raised our shoulders in bewilderment. He turned away from us and shouted at one of his friends who got up and slowly walked over to us. To our utter amazement, he spoke Polish. He asked us to sit down and join them. They were just brewing some hot chocolate; would we like to have some? We were too surprised to say anything, but just nodded our heads in affirmation. The soldiers made room for us, and continued singing.

Our host explained that he was from Upper Silesia, thus his knowledge of Polish language. He told us about disappointingly brief campaign with the Russian here, and he apparently couldn't stop from laughing as he explained that they hadn't even give them a chance to try out their new tanks. He pointed proudly toward the trees, where, hidden from view, stood a large tank. It looked very impressive, and our host was apparently very proud off it. We noticed that these men were dressed differently; they wore black uniforms, and on tips of their they wore a skull and crossed bones. I guessed that they were some kind of special unit. Soon the hot chocolate was ready and our host poured some into cups for us. It was good and we felt very relaxed. We asked if we could see his tank; and he gladly got up and gave us a tour. Once in the tank, he explained the entire operation. He showed us how the turret worked and how the gun was fired. He told us that he was the tank Commander. After the tour, we thank our host for the hot chocolate and the hospitality and waved goodbye to them all. They responded eagerly and shook our hands as we left. This had been a very pleasant encounter. I noticed that the bodies were still there, but now there some trucks parked close by and the bodies were being sprayed with a chemical, apparently to kill off the stench. We hurried on and decided to go downtown.

CHAPTER ELEVEN

German Occupation
Summer 1942

The boulevard was still crowded with marching soldiers and military vehicles. This was so different from the Russian entry into our city. We were much happier now. As we approached City Hall, we couldn't believe our eyes. From the mast were flying two flags, one, as one would expect, the large flag with a large black cross and swastika, the German military flag. But the other one – no, this couldn't be. - I looked at Stefan and he too seemed perplexed. It was the Ukrainian flag, blue and gold. What was the meaning of this? We saw people crowding around some large red posters pasted on the building. Slowly we walked over and read them. They were in Ukrainian. Slowly, to be sure of what I saw, I read its contents. Its bold print stated immediately from the star-Ukraine for Ukrainians – and urged all Ukrainians to join in the fight against the Russians, shoulder to shoulder with the Germans so that we could clear our Homeland of the oppressors and claim our independence. It was signed by "Bandera," the leader of

Ukrainian underground movement. Some people, after reading the posters, walked away briskly, afraid. Others would stare at it and just shake their heads in disbelief. Still others, Ukrainians and Poles alike, would argue about the stupidity and futility of such an announcement.

Stefan and I slowly walked away and started on the way home, preoccupied with the events of the day. I was impressed with the German Army and the Germans themselves. They seemed quite human. I was also impressed with the announcement made by Bandera. I heard his name mentioned many times before, by John and Janusz. They both hated him with a passion and called him a hothead and an opportunist.

I looked at Stefan and said, "Boy, John will really be upset over this announcement." Stefan just shook his head. I couldn't understand why he didn't share my happiness and this hurt me. Then I realized that he too was a member of the Polish resistance movement, and thus was upset over the announcement. As I had anticipated, John was very much upset by the events. The German's entry into the city was one thing, but Bandera's announcement was something entirely different. He was very upset and cursing loudly. Mother became annoyed with him and told him to take a walk and cool off. Angrily he walked out, slamming the door behind him. I laughed, "Mama, he just doesn't like the idea of living in Ukraine." "Shut up, you idiot," Stefan's words struck me with pain. "To hell with you all," I screamed. "I am sick and tired of being treated like a child. Just who do you think you are"? I refused to be pacified by Mother, and continued screaming at Stefan. Then I burst into tears and ran into bedroom. I heard the door open and then close softly. Footsteps approached the bed. Then I felt Stefan's hand on the back of my head. "Sorry, pal," he whispered. I guess I had forgotten that you too are alive, and suffering like the rest of us. You are right. Things were not too good for us before the war," he continued. "But don't you see, they aren't going get any better with hotheads like this Bandera. We must grow up and face the future together. Poles and Ukrainians. This is the only way we will be able to survive. We are really one people now.

His voice was soothing. Possibly he too was considering the future, hoping that the idea of mutual trust and mutual sacrifice would not become clouded with petty strife and thus the significant fight for freedom be lost. Slowly he continued; "No. I'm not ashamed that I'm Polish. As a matter of fact, I make sure that all the people I deal with know this. I'm not a hothead. The only thing I want is freedom; freedom of opportunity to do the things that father and I always wanted. This is what I believe, and as long as I'm able, I'll resist any temptation to abandon this hope"

"You see, I too was very young and, I suppose, still am. But then Janusz came along. He taught me much. My only hope is that there are many people like him still alive today. If his voice is heard, our future in a new Poland will be secured. This is what we must fight for. We must not learn by the mistakes of the past and build our future together." Here he stopped, overcome with emotion. He patted me, again I heard the door close. I was all alone. The events of past two days were so confusing. My head was reeling.

CHAPTER TWELVE

German Occupation
Fall 1942

I don't know how long I stayed there. I was awakened to the present by a commotion in the kitchen. Curious, I got up and went to see what was happening. As I walked in I noticed that John was sitting at the table, his head in his hands, his shoulders shaking violently. He was crying like a baby. Anxiously, I asked what was going on. Stefan asked me to take a walk with him, and we left. For a long time, we walked in silence. All around us was the activity of the German Army; troops, vehicles always on the move. Finally, Stefan spoke, quietly, deliberately, weighing each word; "John has just returned from the two prisons. The Russians have executed most of the prisoners. There were hundreds of dead, tortured horribly and for what? Slowly, he told me what John had seen. We followed a group of people toward the prisons. The doors were wide open and people were going in, some in search of their loved ones, others just out morbid curiosity. Once inside, the view was appalling. The court was lined with dead of bodies. Hundreds of them. Some shot, others horribly mutilated. These were supposedly political prisoners. The Russians had made sure that the victims would not escape and relate to the world how they suffered. In disbelief I followed the crowd, examining the dead, hoping that no one we knew would be there. Unfortunately, there few, some hardly recognizable. The inspection trip was aided by a German Officer who spoke Polish. He quietly pointed out various chambers of torture employed by the NKVD, such as the small cells where inmates couldn't do anything else except stand up. Here they were left until their strength left them and they confessed to the charges preferred against them. Some of the corpses had been burned; apparently, their bodies were first covered with some flammable material and then ignited. In the cellar below the prisons, their bodies stacked high, along the front wall. This is where they were executed, shot down by the Russian machineguns. In other rooms, there bodies of females with portions of their bodies cut off. One pregnant woman had her baby removed through the stomach; and the coldness of death etched in her face and in her eyes expression of horror caused by the pain she had suffered. Then there was a Priest from our Church, crucified to the door, his body badly mutilated. The same conditions existed at the other prisons. Only very few managed to escape the death. Some were feigning the death, hoping to be overlooked, while others, mortally wounded, were overlooked, only to die horrible death few days later.

Stefan had stopped talking and we walked in silence. I was convinced at this moment that I hated the Russians very much and if need be, I would fight them with everything I had. They had ceased to be human to me. No one could perpetrate such monstrous actions and remain human. They had to be destroyed, and I hoped that the German Army would soon avenge the death of the many innocent people who seemed to me to have died so unnecessarily. My mind set on revenge. And so, the days went by. The newspapers were full of stories about executions in the prisons by the retreating Russians. They also continued to proclaim their advance into the Russian plains went on uninterrupted. They were jubilant in their predictions about the collapse of the Russians.

Soon the Front-Line soldiers were gone into Russian interior and their places were taken by SS, Gestapo and the Sonderdienst (Special Units). Again, as before, a local Police Force was established. This time they were again Ukrainians. Numerous edicts were proclaimed by the authorities; no weapons were to be retained by civilians; anyone caught in possession of firearms would be executed; and so on. This was an old story now. And the schools were re-opened and I went back once more. But now we had to learn German.

One of Proclamations stated anyone having a German in the family in the past three generations would qualify as a Volksdeutsche. This of course brought many advantages to those with such a background. It wasn't long before the hated signs appeared everywhere; "Nur fur Deutche and Verbindete", (Only Germans and Allies) only. Even the street cars. had special sections of this nature. It was very perplexing to note that while the section of street cars for the local population was crowded with people hanging out on the steps, the German sections contained only few Germans. Nevertheless, this was one of the edicts, and we had to abide by it.

Soon we found out that the German race considered itself to be superior to our Slavic heritage, and they did everything to keep themselves segregated from us. One thing that was different in this occupation was shortage of food and fuel, and there was no change in sight. We were issued ration cards and it would be utterly impossible to describe how much various portions were assigned to each individual. They were far below normal. Naturally, the black marked flourished once again, driving monetary value down to a point where it became almost worthless. And again, as in the past, bartering became the main source of purchasing power.

I remember John looking sadly at various pieces of furniture which we were forced to barter for food to feed the family. I felt very proud of him in those days. Everything he owned he had worked very hard; and yet, when it became necessary to choose between eating or admiring his material things, he didn't hesitate at all. Even the piano had to go; I remember that we got some potatoes and fresh meat for it. Meanwhile, the German offense in the east continued at a rapid pace. Cities unknown to us before took on real significance – Smolensk, Kiev, Rostov, Stalingrad, Leningrad, and of course, Moscow. The newspapers proclaiming the glory of the German Army; the advance was rapid and some optimists were proclaiming that before the winter season came Russia would collapse. John, of course, didn't share this feeling; he still hated the Germans, and now even more than before. He couldn't forget the fact that they were victors and we the vanquished. Every time we passed a store with a sign in the window "Nur fuhr Deutche and Verbundete" – he would grit his teeth and I could hear him mutter under his breath, "Those bastards."

I must admit it was very difficult to understand how it was possible to have all these fine things for the Germans and their friends in sufficient quantities, when the local population was forced to survive on a starvation diet. Some of the stores were simply beautiful, with all kinds of luxury items in the windows, including white bread! White bread, indeed; it had been a long time since I had this at home. Slowly, I too came to see the difference. I didn't appreciate being second rate just because I was born in Poland. I felt that I was just as good as many of the young Germans who now filled the streets, dressed in their brown shirts with swastika armbands, and their short black pants. Hitler Jugend.

The pattern seemed to be there. During the Russian Occupation it was the Pioniers,; now was Hitler Jugend. There was one exception – the Russians had encouraged everyone to join. They wanted to indoctrinate as many people as possible, particularly the young minds, with their doctrine, whereas the Germans were who could join their ranks. They wanted to keep their "Master Race" pure. This hurt very deeply.

Lwow became a staging area, the main hub of transportation toward East. As a result, the city was always full of soldiers and vehicles, enjoying brief pause before departing eastward. This of course presented many wonderful opportunities for the underground, who had been fairly quiet for a few months, awaiting and examining their new enemy. The nights were once again filled with terror. First, the German soldiers were the unsuspecting victims. accompanied their local girls home, they were met by members of the movement. There followed a short burst from a sawed off shot gun or a sub machinegun, or couple of rounds from a pistol, and it would be allover; the soldiers as well as their girlfriends had paid the price. Ans so it went.

I was still awaiting a chance to join the movement with Bandera. I didn't dare to make my desires known at home for I was, in fact, joining the opposition, and I wasn't quite sure how John and Stefan would react. We talked about the underground activities in school quite openly, always being careful not to mention any names. One learns early when the choice is discretion or death. Finally, one day I was approached by one the senior students who introduced himself as Michael. He indicated that he wanted to talk to me.

After the school, I met him at the main gate. Slowly we started moving toward the street car stop. "Let's walk," he suggested. I shrugged my shoulders and said, "okay." Slowly we walked down the street. In a very quiet voice Michael started talking. As I listened, I looked at him in utter disbelief. He knew everything about my family - my father, John and Stefan being members PPS. Finally came the question. "Why do you want to join Bandera? Why not PPS like the rest of your family?"

It wasn't an easy question to answer. I had often asked the question of myself and the answers weren't quite satisfactory. I just didn't know. I suppose it went back to that Sunday when German troops first marched in and I read the Bandera's Proclamation. It had hit me hard; it had awakened a feeling of patriotism quite unfamiliar to me. Perhaps I longed to become a hero, I didn't know. I replied as best as I could. For a boy of fifteen I tried very hard to sound grown up. I talked earnestly, emphasizing the items outlined in Bandera's proclamation.

Michael didn't say a word. He just listened. After I fell silent, he looked up and said, "I will be in touch with you. Don't discuss this conversation with anyone, particularly with your family." And then he was gone. I continued home alone, very confused and afraid. Was this the right thing to do? Surely, I couldn't hide it from them. Then it struck me that Michael knew everything they found outjhb was to know about us. Was he really on the level or was he working for the Sonderdienst?

The next few days were a nightmare. I kept looking for Michael but he was nowhere to be found. I thought about going to various classes to seek him out, but then, if he was on the level, I would jeopardize my future and chance withe movement. Finally, one day after school he met me at the gate. "Do you have to be home right away?" He asked. When I answered in the negative, he took my hand and directed me down the street. "I am going to take you to a person who is going to talk to you. Based on this interview, you will be either accepted or rejected."

My heart was beating madly; this was my big chance. Apparently, they were satisfied with background information. Now it was up to me to sell myself and to prove to them that I was sincere and that I wanted to do my part. We walked down the street slowly. Michael looked agitated, perhaps even afraid. For the first time, I noticed that he too was very young, no more than seventeen. He kept looking behind him as though expecting someone to be following us. Finally, we made a quick turn into an alley. Here he made me lean against the wall and we waited several minutes to be sure that we were not being followed. Satisfied that the coast was clear, Michael smiled and motioned to me to follow him. We passed several doorways, several yards, and finally descended a long a flight of steps into a cellar. Here we were greeted by a large man. He nodded to Michael and motioned to us to pass. We soon found ourselves in a large room, furnished rather shabbily, with a few small tables and beat up chairs. From the ceiling hung a very small electric light ball. The whole place smelled bad and looked rather eerie. Soon a door opened on the other side and a middle age man walked in. He glanced at us briefly and motioned to us to sit down. Slowly he addressed me in Ukrainian, completely ignoring my friend. "So, you want to join our movement? What can you do? Do you have any special skills, or do you first want to become a hero?"

His tone indicated a sneer. He looked at me, his eyes penetrating mine, deeply, trying to determine what was really going on in my mind, probing, hoping to get at the truth before it was too late. I tried talking, yet I couldn't. I was filled with emotion. I was afraid that they would not give me a chance because of my age and because I really didn't have any special skills. I merely wanted to do what I believed to be right. I wanted to do my share. Slowly I began talking, licking my lips, trying to sound convincing. The man behind the light just looked at me, not saying a word.

I told him how I felt after reading the proclamation; about the anxieties I had felt, wondering what my family would say after my actions became known to them. Finally, I talked about my part in the movement. I knew my limitations, I had no special skills; the only thing I could give was my burning desire to avenge the feelings of suppression and my desire to prove to the Germans that I was good as they. Then I fell silent, casting anxious glances at my inquisitor. His face was expressionless.

"Son, we have been watching you for a long time. Our young friend here brought you to our attention." Here he motioned toward Michael who had been sitting down all this time, just listening.

We have watched you and we have checked into your family background. It is apparent that rest of your family does not share your enthusiasm for the free Ukraine. Why should you? This is one question that bothers me. You just made a fine speech; the words sound very good, and yet, son, you must understand that these are very trying days. We cannot trust anyone fully, on the other hand, can we afford to turn away willing recruits - perhaps young patriots is a better word - just because we don't have all the answers. We must take chances." Here I smiled, for I smelled victory. "However, son," his voice getting harder, "you will get your chance to prove to us that you really believe what you said. Should it become apparent that you were not honest with us, your life will be terminated immediately. The rest is up to you." You now have all answers. If your answer is yes, Michael will take you around and will be your guardian angel for the next few weeks. He will introduce you to other members and teach you the necessary tricks. If, however, you decide that this is not for you, you are free to leave. You must, of course, forget all about this meeting. Should something happen to this place, you will become prime suspect and I don't need to remind you what this would mean.

There really was no decision for me to make. My mind was already made up. I was happy to joint movement and to be given an opportunity to prove myself. Quickly I extended my hand. He grasped it warmly and whispered, "God bless you son." The interview was over. Michael walked out with me. He was all business now. "You will of course, tell no one that you are a member of this group. You will take all orders from me. At first, they will be very simple; as our faith in you grows, you will be given more important assignments. Just remember, we are doing our part and all assignments are important regardless how insignificant they may appear at the time." I noted from his voice that he was happy, satisfied with himself that his protégé had made good. I too was very happy, now I, the last member of my family, and the youngest, would also contribute to the fight against the "Liberators." My mind was too excited to feel any remorse about my action. I had wanted to do this with all my heart and here the opportunity was handed to me. I would not let them down; I resolved to do all that was in my power to do. Michael quietly patted me on the shoulder. "See you soon," he said and turned off.

I was disappointed; I was ready to start my first lesson, ready to attack the German Army single handed. As I walked into the house, I found it difficult to hide my feelings and not to share the news with Stefan. I felt certain that he would understand. But then I remembered my promise and thought I must start on the right foot. Nothing must go wrong. I must make them believe in me. I talked to Mother for a while, asking about John and Stefan. It seemed that they were home less and less each day. Anne had gone out into the country, trying to get some food. In little while, I complained of a headache and went to bed. I had to have time to think things out; this was the beginning of many new adventures. Would I do well? Would I be afraid when the opportunity required me to act without regard for a human life? I just didn't know except that time would tell. Of this I was fully convinced. The next few days went without any news from Michael. I did see him in school during a break, but he completely ignored me. There was nothing to do but wait.

CHAPTER THIRTEEN

German Occupation
Winter 1942

Meanwhile, things were getting quieter at home. Mother had gotten used to idea that the men would be out and would return at all hours of the night. Anne too became resigned to the fact that John would be leading a double life for the duration of the conflict. Thank God, the children; at least they kept Grandmother busy and helped to keep her mind away from worry. I still went to school, and after school we either played soccer or just walked around the city examining things in general.

Sundays were relief. I still belonged to the altar society, and it was a welcome relief to go there. The Priests were so understanding and there was always so much to do. All the boys would relate the latest events and the time would pass by quickly. Then after the last Mass, we would be invited to the garden for coffee and cookies, or when it was too cold, we went into the dining hall. Here, at least, life still went on as it always did; there really was no apparent change.

It was late in the day as I decided to take a walk down the boulevard. As I walked I noticed people crowding around a new proclamation. Curious, I walked over and started reading;

"Effective this date," it read, "all people having Jewish blood in the past three generations will be considered Jews. They will report immediately to the local Gestapo station for issuance of special passes. They will be required to wear an armband on the left arm; it will be white with a blue star of David. Any Jew failing to comply with the Directive will be punished by death; any Aryan willfully harboring such a Jew will also be punished by death."

I walked away with mixed emotions. I had grown up in a neighborhood with Jews, and some of them were my friends. I had often heard some older people talking about Jews, complaining that they had all the property and money while we had nothing. But this was just talk. Now it seemed that the Germans were going to do something about it. The Jews would be forced to earn their money and some menial labor. That wasn't too bad; perhaps this would teach them the facts of life.

When I went home, our next door was with Mother. They were both crying. Somewhat alarmed, I went to the kitchen to check on what was going on. It was almost time for supper, so Mother asked the neighbor to call her son, Herbert, to join us for supper. Mr. Schwartz went out and returned few minutes later with Herbert. They were both visibly shaken. By this time, John and Stefan had come in and we all sat down at the table. During the meal, Herbert started to talk about the recent order to register and wear armbands. "This is merely the beginning," he said. "Soon, we will be ordered into a crowded ghetto, stripped of all property and finally put to death. This is what Hitler really wants. He wants to destroy the Jews; this he stated in his book "My Kampf." Herbert was about Stefan's age, and I had known him all my life. His parents owned a small grocery downstairs and I remember that during the thirties, when there was no money they would not sell us any food on credit. Now times have changed. I could not feel any compassion for them.

I remember seeing Jews kissing Russian tanks when they first arrived; they were happy to get rid of our capitalists and join the regime that proclaimed that we were all equal. Well, things have changed once more. They had had two years of quiet; now it was their turn for a little misery. Mrs. Schwartz just kept crying and nodding her head to her son's remarks. Mother tried to quiet them down, saying that all this was just a rumor; that things changed from day to day. "Don't worry. Everything is going to be alright." I stole a glance at John and Stefan. They were totally indifferent. I felt certain that they too remembered the days when we didn't have any money or food and the fine people, now begging for mercy, refused to be bothered by our plight. I could not wait for the supper to end.

In the next few days it seemed silly at first to see all Jews wearing armbands. They were apparently very self-conscious off the band, and people kept sneering and laughing at them. A few days later, as I come back from school, I noticed a group of young SS men at the corner of St Paul street and Lyczakowski Blvd. They were standing in a group, just laughing, and nearby was a large group of young Poles. Everyone seemed to be waiting for something to happen. Soon it dawned on me that this was the time for Jews to return from their work details. As I approached the group, I saw a young Jew wearing an armband, afraid to face the SS men, crossing the street. "Hey, Jude, komme here," one of them shouted at him. Petrified, the young man stopped and slowly and slowly walked back toward the group. I froze to the ground, unable to move. I knew something horrible was about to take place. Slowly the young Jew the group of SS men, his identification card in his right hand. One of the group took his papers, looked them over and started to hand them back to him. His arm extended only halfway, forcing the Jewish boy to come closer. As soon as he took a couple of steps, he was hit full in the mouth. Then they were all hitting him. I shall never forget this sight. The boy was unable to free himself from the group, and fell to the ground as they continued to kick him, in the head, in the groin, anywhere. The SS Men just laughed. His body was a bloody mess. Slowly, half-blind, he rose to his feet and started running. Now the group of young Poles joined the fun. They pounced on like wild animals and soon he was down again, and many feet were kicking him unmercifully. The SS men enjoyed the show immensely; waving their arms and shouting encouragements. Soon the body ceased to move. I couldn't see for the tears my eyes, and I ran home like one possessed. This cannot be, I kept repeating to myself. We are not animals, we are human beings. How can we act like this? Quickly I ran upstairs and into the bedroom where I threw myself on the bed, sobbing violently.

John followed me into the bedroom and sat down beside me. "What is the matter, son?", he asked quietly. Sobbing, I told him about the scene I had just witnessed. "John those our own people. How can you talk about a future in a new Poland when people like this live among us? What kind of future will we have? What has this war, this miserable war done to us?" "Son, we are the worst animals that ever lived. Sometimes it is necessary for a self-preservation. At other times, it is necessary because of what we believe in. Do you think we enjoy hunting down Germans or, for that matter, our own people who have sold their souls to the enemy? Every time I see a dead body I cannot help but wonder who he is and what his family will say. Did he really deserve to die, or did he just die because he happened to be in wrong place at wrong time? Son, this war is miserable and I hope and pray to God that when this is over that ourselves we will have preserved enough decency so that we will be to return to a normal once more."

One day after school Michael came up to me and said curtly "Let's go." Without a word, I followed his footsteps. We walked briskly and soon found ourselves in front of an old building.

Michael through the door and motioned for me to follow. We went through a dark corridor and soon were descending steps into a cellar. It was extremely dark and it took some time before my eyes became accustomed to the darkness so that I could observe various objects on the way. After few minutes, we approached a door. Michael stopped and knocked three times, paused, then knocked twice more. The door opened, revealing a small room with couple of tables, surrounded by chairs. At least here we had light. The room was already filled with boys varying in ages. From fourteen to eighteen. They all looked at us, indifferently, curiously. Behind the table stood a fairly man of, I would say, about thirty-eight to forty years old. As soon as walked in he motioned to two empty chairs.

"Gentlemen, you all Michael. The boy with his is George, his protégé. This is his initial meeting with us and it will be awhile before we will be able to judge him; thus, accept him as one of us until he proves himself different. "I looked around the room, and gazed at the eyes that were all staring at me, trying to determine who I was and what I would do. I felt certain that my face turned crimson. I panicked for a while, but then, I had asked for this. I stared back at them defiantly. I would prove myself once the time arrived for it.

The leader introduced himself for my benefit as Lieutenant Andrew. Then he continued; "Gentlemen, you are all aware that the Germans are breaking the promises made to us. The Gestapo and all other special units are on alert to apprehend all resistance fighters." He placed the emphasis on "All." I need not remind you that we must continue to fight back. It will be a long war for us, but we cannot let up now. There is too much at stake. We too have a chance for freedom once this war is over. It has been a long time since this general area belonged to a sovereign Ukraine. "Here his voice shook with emotion as he continued: "and we shall not give up the fight regardless of the price."

I looked around me. Everyone in the room was tensely watching the Lieutenant; no one took his words lightly. They all knew the price. How can people change so much? The thought flashed through my mind. These are boys here, some my age. Is this fair? The Lieutenant was still talking. "The orders for future actions will be given to individual cell leaders as soon as we break up, and the normal procedure will apply. You will depart from here through the rear door, two at a time. It should be dark before we start. Remember, in case of capture, it is essential that at least one of you get away so that the rest can be warned; we can then move to the alternate meeting place. God speed!"

Lieutenant Andrew called us to the table. His hand was extended and he warmly shook hands with me. "George, glad to have you with us. Michael will be your guardian angel for the next few weeks. He will teach you need to know; other things you will pick up yourself or they will come to you when the time comes. Remember, son, you have been given ample opportunity to change your mind; now, you cannot quit!" Here his voice was hard. "You already know too much and we cannot afford to have you leave us. I hope that that you understand this." I shook my head in the affirmative.

Yes, I often thought about. What about the day, should it come, when Mother would find out and beg me to stop? What would I do then? Would I say no and break her heart, adding to her already deep worries about Stefan and John? But it was already too late. I made my decision and would stick to it. On the way home, Michael told me about the movement, and about himself. He was sixteen years old; his father had executed by the Russians as an enemy of the State. He was the only son, and his mother knew what he was doing and prayed for him. He was one of the leaders of the younger groups. Their mission, and mine now, was to carry messages, and occasionally, cut telephone wires.

Just like Stefan, I thought wryly. We share the same beliefs and the same ideals, the same planes of actions, and yet, will these two movements join shoulder to shoulder when the time comes? This question always bothered me. And so, I asked Michael; "should I quit the altar society now that I am a member of Ukrainian movement?" He looked at me and said with conviction; "no, you must not change your activities in any way that would attract attention; just go and be yourself. If people are accustomed to seeing you in certain places, don't change that. That is the first lesson. You must learn to lead a double life. You are a resistance fighter now, but you will fight only when it becomes necessary. In the meantime, you must act as though nothing has happened." He then told me that in our little group there six boys, all my age. Their names were not important. "They were all in the room with us. They know you now and they will be watching every step you take. God, help you should the reports reaching me indicate something irregular. Again, this insane distrust? What must I do to prove to them that I'm sincere and am doing this because I want to and because I believe in it.

"You will be contacted by one of the boys. He will direct you to an address, you will have a sealed envelope which you will deliver and ask no questions. In the event of something unusual at the address, you will keep the package and return home. You will be contacted the following day to dispose of the envelope." Then he smiled; "that's is enough for one day. Don't be afraid." Here his voice grew soft. "We must be careful. You will understand when you are with us a little longer." We shook hands and parted.

For the next few days I was on pins and needles, eagerly awaiting a visitor. But the days just went on and on with no one approaching me. I grew restless, hoping that Stefan would stay so we could go out and just wander around together. My God, it has been a long time since we even talked. I wandered what Stefan was doing these days. I knew that was reemployed by the radio station in the city. Of course, the station was run by the Gestapo now. What a twist; if they only knew that at night he operated slightly different radio station, one of his own, talking with London. On the other hand, it was better that they didn't know about its existence, better for all of us.

CHAPTER FOURTEEN

German Occupation
Winter 1942

The following Sunday I asked Father Leon to take a walk with me in the church garden for my question. Slowly, we walked around the fruit trees, silently at first, as I tried to find the proper words for my questions. "Father Leon," I started, "is it wrong to hate a person just because of his religion?" Before he answered, I asked another question. "Father, why is it that the Jews are being punished so severely by the Germans?" Slowly, Father Leon formulated his answers; he apparently knew that more questions would be forthcoming. "Yes, it is wrong to hate any person, for whatever reason. Secondly, the Jews are being punished by the Germans because of the Nazi belief that they are impure and the source of all the evils that have ever befallen Germany. Hitler rose to power on this doctrine, and, as he stated in his book, 'Mein Kamp', the Jews must be expelled from the German Society." Then I told him about the incident of several days past; about the young boy who was coming home from a labor detail, not really anticipating the calamity that would befall him that night. He had given up his life because he wore an armband with a star of David and because some German SS men decided to make fun of him. I also told him how I felt, witnessing this murder. "Father, how can our own people participate in such things? We have grown up with many Jews; of course, some of them are bad, but so what? We are all far from perfect. How can we, who have suffered so much already because of the war join this monstrosity and pair up with our oppressor in oppressing others just because of their religion?"

My voice shook with emotion. I couldn't shake from my mind the sight of that bloodied body lying in the gutter, begging for mercy. I just kept asking myself why, repeatedly. Father Leon led me to a bench under a tree and we sat down. "Son, this is war. You will see things that will turn your stomach before it is over. You will first become sick and will later be unmoved by the sight of death and of suffering. You will become very selfish, interested only your own survival. We are all human, placed here for a purpose. Who knows what our goal in life really is? Perhaps we will all perish before the of this war.

"One thing we must not forget, however. Our stay here on earth is temporary and very short in the fact of eternity. We must retain our sense of decency and our faith in God. We must turn to Him for guidance when we become confused, for only He knows our ultimate destination. No one here is a saint; we all make mistakes, and therefore we must pray. We must live by a Christian code, 'Love thy neighbor'.

"Yes, I know you want to fight the Germans, pay them back with misery for the misery that they inflicted on us. But is it really the way? What can be accomplished by fighting fire with fire? We must grasp our faith as a shield and keep our hearts and minds pure." I became very confused at this stage. I know what a good Catholic, or any good Christian, for that matter, should do. But how can one go on believing in the doctrine of charity when everyone around is suffering; when people are dying simply because they happen to be there? My mind closed to Father's words, PRAY AND TRUST GOD'.

I knew then that I had to go on with the underground. There was the way. A tooth for a tooth an eye for an eye. Resolution brought calm and I thanked father Leon for his time. We walked back to the church; I noticed that he was smiling. "Good," I thought; I hope that he will never fine so remote that he never reached me that day.

Several days later I received my first assignment. I was to deliver an envelope to an address in the city. I was very excited and happy. Everything went according to schedule. I met my contact at the proper time. As we passed each other, he bumped into me, we switched newspapers and I was on my way. It was early in afternoon and the streets were crowded with German Soldiers. I imagined at first that they were all following me, just waiting for me to stop at this address before arresting me. How silly!

I arrived at the proper house, looked around very carefully to see if I was being followed, walked rapidly to the mail box and deposited the newspaper. My job was over. I returned home. I enjoyed the feeling of accomplishment and I must have looked very happy for Mother inquired as to the reason for my exuberance. I was in a wonderful mood.

Days went by without any further activity on my part. They seemed to be so remote from us then. The German Army was still advancing very rapidly through the Russian plains. The city was still full of soldiers and military equipment; the underground had slowed down its activities somewhat; the black market was flourishing and food was getting shorter and shorter.

CHAPTER FIFTEEN

German Occupation
Summer 1943

Yet another Proclamation which announced that in order preserve coal for the war effort, the lights would have to be turned off during certain hours, from nine in the evening to six in the morning. This wasn't too bad; the summer time days were long and we really didn't need any lights. But with fall approaching rapidly, the hours had to be extended, first eight, then seven pm.

Soon we started during candles, for the Germans had inspectors checking the houses. They would walk and check the meters. The report would show in which apartment the meter was moving, indicating that the electricity was being utilized during the curfew, and the guilty party would pay a fine in addition to losing the use of electricity completely. Soon the same thing was made applicable to water. During certain hours, no water would be available for use. I remember one day Mother forgot to shut off a spigot to the cold-water system, and the next morning when the water was turned on at the water works, we had water all over apartment, six inches deep. Poor Mother, she was so embarrassed.

The proclamations against Jews came now in rapid succession. They were to give up all their properties, with the state generously taking over all their material wealth. They were ordered to report labor battalions for work; failure to do so meant a further cut in rations, already below the level we were getting. As days grew cold, I used to see them, wearing their armbands, working on menial jobs; poor and ragged, carrying tin cans for their food. They were totally oblivious of our stares; by this time, they were becoming accustomed to their situation; just hoping to left alone to live out their misery But the Germans had different ideas. The final blow came when the Order was read advising the Jews that they had something like a month to move into a ghetto. Here the human greed was at its worst. The only thing the Jews were interested in at this time to convert anything they might have in a way of property into money, preferably gold or American dollars.

The Black Market flourished. Everyone was buying everything they could from the Jews, at ridiculous prices, knowing full well that they had had to sell for the Germans had assigned each a certain poundage that they could retain. Besides, the quarters in the ghetto would be extremely crowded and they really have no use for furniture or any items of luxury. I remember Mrs. Schwartz coming over to see Mother, giving her some things, Mother buying others, hoping in some fashion to help her out. I remember the meal she had with us not too long before and I felt ashamed of my thoughts. Now I felt sorry for her, hoping that she would not suffer too much and perhaps might, by some miracle, escape with her family from the end that she and her son knew coming their way.

When the deadline arrived, all Jews were in the ghetto. It was situated in the worst section of town, and thousands of Jews were confined in small area. The congestion defied the imagination. The ghetto was surrounded by a barbwire fence, and the SS, the

Sonderdienst (Special Units wearing Black Uniforms), and the Ukrainian Police provided the security forces to control the area. Every day the work battalion would leave the ghetto to work in the city, and at night they would return to their miserable existence.

The winter was now in full swing and it was getting cold. The fuel shortage didn't help any either. In school awe had to sit in class with our coats on, for there was no heat; and at home all fuel conserved to cook meals and heat only one room. When the time for bed came, we ran into rooms, darting under the bedcovers with a hot water bottle to keep our feet warm. At the front, the German offensive had come to a halt. The German troops were approaching Moscow, but they were unable to move ahead because of severe winter. Soon, trains loaded down with German wounded began converging on the city. The wounded were transferred into special streetcars to transport them to the military hospitals.

The caliber of the German soldier had changed noticeably. The young care free boys that we had seen not too long ago walking with their shirt sleeves rolled up were gone, replaced by the men who had already had seen too much suffering. These men were older, weary of this war, hoping that it would not go on much longer, yet afraid to say so. They were sick of seeing what happened to the civilian population. They were sick with the worry about their own families suffering from the bombings by the Allies. Yes, Germany was having its problems.

As though things weren't already bad enough, the Underground now really started its activity against the Germans. One Sunday afternoon we were sitting in movie theater, watching a movie, when all sudden the lights went on. Down the aisle came young men dressed in civilian clothing, carrying automatic weapons. From the rear of theater came a loud voice, first in German, then in Polish, advising the customers that the movie was being temporarily interrupted to permit members of PPS to collect monetary contributions for prosecution of the war against Germany. There were several German soldiers in the audience; they wisely remained calm, knowing full well that the slightest move on their part would meant death. Quickly the wart was passed from row to row and the people were willing contributors, visibly enjoying the spectacle. Soon, the lights went out again and the movie continued. The Germans immediately left the theater, to report the incident, I suppose, though by now this type of occurrence was not uncommon.

Now the Underground units out in the field resumed their activities against German Army also. Trains were being blown periodically, and though the Germans were doing all they could to patrol the tracks, it just a sheer impossibility. It appears everyone was working for, or at least with, the underground. The Germans began forcing the local population to ride first three cars, immediately behind the locomotive, thus hoping to discourage the underground from attacking the trains and killing their own people. But as always, there was a solution for this; delayed bombs were put in the use and they did they damage superbly. Army trains were equipped with special cars in front and rear, each equipped with machine-guns and small canons to fight off any attacks from partisans. Still the attacks continued.

No one was save from partisans. They would lie hidden, and as the trains approached, they would fire from their hidden positions for three or four minutes, then disappear. In most cases, attempts were made to destroy the locomotive thus forcing the train to stop. When the troops dismounted, and accepted the challenge, the partisan would quickly depart, their objective achieved. Another locomotive destroyed, another train damaged; another group of German soldiers exposed to the fright of having to deal with the partisans, thus contributing to their miseries while in this occupied territory.

In the city, the reign of terror increased also, and no German soldier was safe from a bullet from unseen assassin. The guards at various installations were shot at from fast moving cars; while younger contingent of the underground practiced throwing hand grenades into crowded mess halls.

By this time, I felt like a veteran, for I too participated in missions of this sort. At first I was sick, but then I grew reckless and careless about my actions. The battle was on and somebody would have to be hurt. Better than me, seemed the right motto.

CHAPTER SIXTEEN

German Occupation
Winter - Spring 1942

The Germans retaliated rapidly and viciously. Twenty prominent local members of intelligentsia were arrested and held
as hostages. Proclamations were issued listing the names of all
hostages and stating that if single German soldier is killed by the
underground within the next thirty days, these hostages would be
executed.

It was a bitter pill to swallow for the leaders of the movement,
but they really had no choice. The fight had to go on. And so,
decision was made to go onto ignore the ultimatum presented by
the Germans. As promised, the first execution took place in the
early spring. The people were advised by radio and in the papers
as to the time and place of the execution. It would be held at high
noon on April 3rd. The twenty hostages would then be executed
because of the crimes committed by the underground.

I didn't know anyone on the list personally, but some names
sounded familiar, all prominent people. Finally, the day came,

April 3rd. I used some excuse to get away from the school, and made my way slowly toward the city square. This was the place where the Germans had decided to hold their show. I arrived at the scene at approximately 11:30 am. A large crowd had already gathered there and as I moved about, I recognized few familiar faces. We completely ignored each other, preoccupied each with his own thoughts, wondering about the share of guilt we shared in this execution.

The Germans were really putting on a show. The area was completely sealed off with SS and Gestapo. There were even light machine guns mounted on the roof tops, apparently anticipating or discouraging any desperate move on the part of the underground. I walked around to the south side of the city hall, and there they were - five gallows. To the right of them a man-made mound, approximately five feet high and forty feet long. Here the others will be shot, I thought. I quickly glanced at my watch; 11:45 am; it won't be long now. The Germans were taking their places in the scene; the show would soon begin.

There were several trucks and vans parked around the gallows; I guessed that some of them contained the hostages. At 11:55 am, a platoon of Sonderdienst soldiers dressed in battle gear, goose-stepped to the front of the gallows as drum and bugle groups took their positions. At precisely twelve noon, the bugle sounded a note; a German SS Officer walked up the microphone. In his right hand, he held a piece of paper. Slowly he began reading in German. Next to him stood an interpreter, dressed in SS uniform, translating each sentence into Polish. The list of crimes committed by the underground was long and included numerous attacks on the German military. The names of the German soldiers killed during the probation period was read, followed by those of hostages. Of these, five were to be hanged; the others to be executed by the firing squad. The Officer ended by saying that the blame for this necessary bloodshed was squarely on the shoulders of the underground. "The German authorities have given them ample time to decide which way to act. They have made their choice and because of it, twenty people will die today. Others will follow, should the assassinations of German soldiers continue". Here he read a list of twenty additional hostages that had been taken during the previous night. And again, the list included some of the best-known people in Lwow.

The speech has ended. The officer with outstretched arm, shouted, "Heil Hitler," and did about face. Now another Officer took over. His saber outstretched in his right hand, barked commands to the assembled platoon of SD men. Ten men came forward and advanced toward the gallows. Soon they were mounting the high steps, two men per gallows. There was another command. The drums were beating constant sound, as though at a funeral. The doors of one the closest van opened and the first hostage stepped down to face the sun light. I noticed that his eyes squinted at first, then he looked around at the crowd. His eyes turned to the right towards the gallows and a shudder shook his shoulders as he was struck with the realization of what was facing him now, fully aware that this was the end, that he would not live to see the end of the struggle. For him the war was over and perhaps he wondered why. I knew how he felt, but I wondered if he was glad or sad, or perhaps angry that he had to die. I hoped that he would understand our position. We really didn't have any choice. I hoped he knew that.

Another command. The procession came to a halt at the foot of the gallows. Another command. Each hostage was led all the way to the top. Slowly the men were turned around with their arms bound behind them. They looked at the crowd. There was complete silence. What were they thinking, I wondered? Are they still hoping for a miracle that would rescue them from all this? The hostages were handed black hoods, which were placed over their heads. I couldn't look any longer, and I cast my eyes toward the ground. Then I heard screams, and the crowd gasped as one. When I looked towards the gallows I saw five bodies, swinging on the end of ropes, still kicking. Their necks were all twisted. Soon even the kicking stopped.

Now the crowd was sobbing violently, fully realizing that these people had died and not really knowing fully why. All around the people were screaming and crying; some even got sick. The drum continued their death music, as fifteen more hostages were led out of the vans. They moved towards the sound, their arms bound behind their backs. As they walked they looked at the bodies still hanging from the gallows. Some started to sob, just crying and feeling sorry and perhaps afraid to die. Others among them seemed to calm down as they lifted their heads unafraid and moved briskly forward, knowing that the end was near, determined to die as a man, unafraid, hoping that this would somehow add to the glory of their fight.

Again, the Officer approached the row of the hostages, offering each of them a black hood, which several proudly refused. Officer moved and barked a command. A squad of SS men raised their rifles, against the background, chanting their death melody. Another command. The rifles were now leveled. Fearfully I looked at the condemned men. Those with hoods over their heads, just waiting for the bullets to end their existence; those without them, just staring calmly at the soldiers. Another command. The shots silenced the drums for a second. Again, came a sob from the crowd. Where fifteen men stood before, there were now fifteen bodies lying down, some writhing in blood, others perfectly still in death. Again, the Officer moved forward slowly, this time a pistol in his hand, moving from body to body administrating the coup de grace. He stopped, reloaded and continued.

Now the show was over. I glanced at my watch, 1:15 - only hour plus had passed and twenty people had given up their lives. I hoped it was not in vain. I noticed that my eyes were filled with tears, but I could not feel shame. How could one look at this spectacle without feeling anything? Slowly, I looked around me trying to memorize everything in sight. The SS men were still there with their mighty machine guns still mounted on the roof tops. On the ground, the vans began to move out, empty. The loud speakers proclaimed first in German and then Polish, that the dead bodies would be left on the gallows for the remainder of the day, as a reminder to the to the population that the Germans meant business and wanted underground activity stopped.

The bodies of persons executed by the firing squad were placed in the trucks to be taken to the cemetery for burial. I noticed that the priest was allowed to say a prayer over the bodies. The crowd was now slowly breaking up, most of the people crying, hoping now to get away from the square as fast as the legs would carry them. I walked slowly toward a street car stop to ride home. I felt completely numb. I felt somehow responsible, or at least partially, for the execution. I wondered if we were doing the right thing. I wondered if it was worth the effort. Could we accomplish enough to justify the killing? Questions like this were going through my mind.

It won't be long now, I thought, before the darkness and a will go out ignoring the curfew, to write our little messages foe the population. "Remember April 3rd 1942, the legend of Lwow." Someday in the future these people will be vindicated, of this I was certain. But right now, I felt completely lost. I hoped that we could accomplish enough to testify the death. I felt that from now on, it really wouldn't matter. I think part of me died that day, and the rest was immaterial. The only thing that mattered now was to repay them - doubly if possible.

That night we went out equipped with chalk, writing on everything that was available, bringing a message to the people that the underground knew that these people were executed and that others were awaiting the same fate unless the underground gave up. And yet, the stakes were much too high. The struggle had to go on. The only thing we could do was to convert this date into a memorial, trying to bring home the message that the front was no longer somewhere in Russia, but right here.

The night passed without incident. Several times I had to dodge German patrols, but that was all. The following day I proudly surveyed our work. Everywhere you looked, there was a sign written in large letters on the wall - "Remember April 3, 1942 - the legend of Lwow.

CHAPTER SEVENTEEN

German Occupation
Spring 1943

Several days later returning from school, I noticed that Anne and Mother were both in the kitchen crying. I asked what was wrong, and Anne said that John had been missing for two days now. Nobody knew where he was. She called the radio station several times but we weren't at work. The only alternative was that he had gone with the unit somewhere on an important mission, something that couldn't wait. But that too was unlikely, for he would have violated the cardinal rule of the underground, leading a double life.

I sought out Stefan and begged him to do something, to get hold of Janusz and start looking for John. Stefan returned couple of hours later, weary and worried, saying only that the underground knew nothing off his whereabouts, but were declaring an emergency, expecting the worst.

Later in the evening, we received word from John's boss at the station saying that he thought he knew where John might be found.

This German was very fond of John and was upset over his disappearance. Two more days went without any word. Finally, the master from the station called and told us that John has been arrested and charged with crimes against the state. We were all aghast; it would now be but a matter of days before we were all taken in. Of this we were certain.

That night, Master Sergeant Loeb came over to the house. We asked him to sit down and have a sandwich and a cup of coffee with us; as we all sat down around the table he began with his findings. It seemed that John had become upset over something and had gone to a bar where he had several drinks and became quite drunk. He blamed the Germans for the execution of the hostages. His criticism was overheard by some policemen on duty, and soon the Gestapo was called in and John was led away. The personnel at the radio station done all they could to locate to find him, and finally located him at the jail on Kazmieczoska street. Various attempts were made to real him, but all to avail. Finally, the Captain in charge of radio station appealed to the Gestapo to have John released, stating that he was a good employee and essential to continued efficient operation of the station. It was agreed that he would be released in the custody of the personnel at the radio station. Here, Master Sargent Loeb looked around us hoping that we understood what was involved. He and all the others at the radio station stood to lose everything should something wrong happen. Then he continued, saying that John would be released the following morning. We all cried with joy and thanked him and the entire personnel at the radio station.

That night in bed, I couldn't sleep. Again, I was confused. How can I hate them all without reservation when there some decent people left even among them? They did not have to go to all that trouble for John and yet they did. Why? Softly I cried out to Stefan; he answered immediately, as he too was apparently unable to sleep, fighting his conscience. I came over to his bed and sat on the edge.

"Stefan, what are we going to do?" I inquired. "Will we be able to continue with what we have doing for the past several months, or do you think we will be watched too closely? Do you feel that we can afford to take the chance and continue our work?" He just shook his head and said: "I just don't know." I am not going to say anything until I see John." I agreed. We really didn't have any choice; for not only would be endangering our family; we would be endangering everyone connected with the movement if we were to be placed under surveillance by the Gestapo. We just must wait and see what happens.

The next morning John came home in a German Staff car furnished by the radio station. He had been missing only four days, but I shuddered when I first saw him. He looked horrible. He must have lost at least ten or fifteen pounds. His face was all black and blue from the beating he received. His eyes were sunken deeply into his head, and his hair looked much grayer than before. He must really have gone through hell in these few days. The Germans who brought him home were very understanding; they just accompanied him to the door ad left, wanting to leave us alone to discuss the events of the day's past. Quietly we all joined in welcoming him home. He was visibly shaken and he looked very strange. We all sat around the table for coffee and sandwiches, waiting for John to relate the activities of the past few days. His face was very thoughtful, concentrating on these events, hoping to tell everything. Quietly he began.

"After witnessing the execution of the hostages, I felt sick. I had to go someplace and drown this feeling of shame and sorrow. I stopped at the first bar I could find. Quickly I downed few drinks, and then I couldn't stop; I was furious - with myself, with the war, and most of all, with the Germans. "Apparently, I became quite drunk and talkative; I remember several people coming by my table to suggest that perhaps I had better go home. But this only encouraged me to drink more. Finally, several policeman came over and asked me to go outside. Once outside, I noticed a German patrol car. They were waiting for me. I panicked and hoped that I didn't have any weapons on me. Thank God I was clean." I was taken to the prison and assigned to a cell. The first night was rather quiet; I don't remember much of it other than the fact that I was glad to get to bed. I shared cell with several others, approximately fifteen to be exact, all of them policy prisoners. Five or six of them would walk into the cell and select their victim. Then they placed a sack over his head and proceeded to beat him up. I was lucky; the first two nights I managed to escape. But the third night they caught up with me. Again, we were counting the doors; then it was our turn. All six of them walked in, and as we cringed against the wall, each one going that they would escape, they just looked around. Then the selection was made, and before I knew it, I had a sack over my head and the beating had started. I don't know how long it went on. I remember falling and they started on me with their boots.

Anne was sobbing quietly. I prayed to God that they would finish the job right then and there, for I knew that if ever came out of this alive I would have no mercy on those bastards whatsoever. In the past, I had given many of them another chance, but not ever again. As long as they are Germans, they will pay, and they will pay dearly. By following night, I was just about out of my mind, and I decided to end it all. I tore my shirt into shreds and made rope out it. As soon as everyone was asleep, I tried hanging myself. Fortunately, I suppose, I was discovered by my cell mates who cut me down, or rather tore me down without calling the guards. You know the rest.

For a long time, we sat at the table, discussing our future plans, this time totally oblivious of the presence of Anne and Mother. Something had to be done. We had to have a plan of action that would satisfy everyone. Stefan and I discussed our anxieties about German surveillance with John. He merely laughed and said," we will have to be doubly careful, that is all."

CHAPTER EIGHTEEN

German Occupation
Spring of 1943

With spring in the offing, talk of new German offense started once more. Things weren't going too well on eastern front these days. Slowly the German tide was stopped, and then turned back. First came withdrawals from Odessa and other distant places and then the capture of Moscow a legend or a dream. The Germans were done. They apparently knew this, for their activities against the Jews doubled in intensity. Many evenings we could see white cloud over ghetto and smell of burning flesh.

The ghetto was overcrowded and the Germans decided to do something about it. The executions of Jews went on daily basis in the nearby quarries outside the city limits. It was easy to tell. Jews were transported in open trucks, lying flat on the floor, covered with tarpaulins, while on the cab of the truck sat an SS man with machine pistol. As the news from the front continued to show drastic situation, the trucks with Jews were seen making trips toward the quarries. The Jews were taken there for the final solution. It made no difference who they were; men, women and children. They were rounded up, and as soon as the truck was filled up, they were taken away.

At the quarry, located about 10 miles east of the city, the trucks would pull in. The Jews were ordered out, told to strip to the skin and hand over all their wordy possessions. Naked, they were marched to a spot, given shovels and told to start digging their grave. Upon completion of digging the trench, a board was thrown over across it and the Jews were told to stand on the board and face the troops; the SS men mowed then down with machine pistols. The next contingent would be ordered to cover the bodies with sand, regardless of whether they were dead or not, then ordered to stand on the edge of the pit and face the troops to be mowed down. This activity was witnessed by factions of the underground; this had to recorded for the posterity and pictures of the executions were taken, to be smuggled out the West. The world had to know. This slaughter could not go unnoticed - and unpunished. Eventually, someone would have to pay.

Few days later Stefan and I went for a walk. It was a nice spring day so we decided to walk and enjoy our company. Before long, we spotted a group of people crowding around a new Proclamation pasted on the wall. It was typical red poster. However, as we approached the scene, we saw some people laughing and clearing the area, as we read the proclamation, we realized that it was not what it seemed to be; it was a proclamation but not by the Government but by the Underground informing the public of the genocide committed by the Germans on the Jewish people; citing of the ghettos and the location of the quarry where the crimes were committed. Soon we heard the sirens of Police car arriving with button in hand dispersing the crowd; they came prepared with buckets of black paint which they used to cover the Proclamations. We read enough, so we quietly abandoned the site walking toward a street car stop a few blocks ahead. Arriving home, we found our family getting ready for supper.

Stefan and I were very anxious to share our news with John; after the supper, we immediately cornered John and told him what we saw. He looked at us with grin and said; "I guess my message got trough." He then told us he received a package from Janush; a film detailing the executions at the quarry. He didn't say how, but confirmed that the film was received in London, our Government in exile, and they have authorized the Proclamation to inform general of atrocities being committed by the Germans who were to destroy all evidence of the Jewish Final solutions.

On the Russian front things were getting desperate for the Germans. Now that the Russian knew that there would not be attack from Japan, they transferred the Elite 3 Divisions of Siberians, who were guarding the border, to spearhead the actions against the Germans. We could see this in the city when the Main Street car lines were shut down for the military use for hours at the time. Germans were using street cars converted into ambulances shuttling arriving wounded soldiers to local hospital where they would be examined and transferred to a military hospital in Germany, For us it was bad news and good news. Good news, the Germans were on the ropes, bad news, the Russians were coming. At home, things were subdued except for John. He was elated, the Germans were in full retreat and he loved it. But what about the Russians, we asked. We worry about them when they arrive, he said. I looked at Stefan and he just shook his head.

CHAPTER NINETEEN

German Occupation
Spring 1943

Several days before Easter, we were out of school and enjoying the vacation again. The weather was fine and there was time for soccer. However, this Easter proved to be very memorable. Everyone was celebrating; the entire contingent of Germans in the city must have been drunk, and we too had several drinks at home and were getting very happy. The hands of clock were nearing nine in the evening when suddenly, all hell broke loose. The air was filled with the sound of falling bombs, screams, and the rapid fire of machine pistols. I suppose we all reacted with fear, and before we knew what was happening, I was in the cellar anxiously awaiting arrival the rest of the family.

Meanwhile, on the streets above us we could hear screams in German and firing of small automatic weapons. The heavier flak joined in, but it was very sporadic. Then overhead we could hear sounds of engines, and the old sound of falling bombs. They were exploding all around us, and some of them sounded as though they were exploding upstairs, so near they were falling. Then I remembered that their trucks parked all round us. This was what the aircraft were after.

The sound of bombs continued, getting louder by the minute. Soon, a small boy, about six years old started praying; "Our Father, who art in heaven.....". His mother became quite hysterical and started to scream that the end of world was coming to us; that we were about to pay our sins. She urged us to join her son in prayer. Some older man told her to shut her mouth, but the women went over to comfort her. Soon, her hysteria spent, she hunched there sobbing very quietly.

Wave after wave of planes returned and the sound of bombs continued for hours. Once, in the lull between the waves of attacking aircraft, some drunk walking down the street was heard screaming at the top his voice, "Mother, listen to those eggs falling down."

It was early in the morning before any one of us dared to walk upstairs to see what had happened. Our apartment was filled with broken glass; we didn't have a window left in the house. All around us the buildings and trucks were burning, while below the military were running around chasing God only knows what.

The war had finally returned to us. God, it has been such a long time since she had experienced anything of this sort, that we had completely forgotten that there was a war in the world. Now it was brought home to us all too well. We had no doubt that it was Russian aircraft that had attacked the unsuspecting city. The timing couldn't have been better. Everyone was drunk celebrating Easter, and Russian had sneaked in behind a flight of German Stukas returning from a mission on the Easter Front. Just as soon as they landed, the Russians bombed the airfield and proceeded to bomb the city. Nobody doubted that we could expect much of the same frequently from now on. In the daytime, the Germans continued their persecution of the Jews, and at night the Russians continued their bombardment of the city. The war had returned to Lwow once more.

The situation at the Eastern Front was getting worse by the day, and the Germans were withdrawing along the entire front. The communiques from the front all read about the same; "German Forces have abandoned the city and are withdrawing to previously selected positions. The enemy suffered heavy casualties". Finally came the news from Stalingrad. The offensive had collapsed and the German Sixth Army, commanded by General von Paulus surrendered to the Russians. The authorities declared three days of mourning for the brave heroes of Stalingrad. All movie houses, opera, and all bars with music were silenced for three days. Everyone knew that was the end. Just like Napoleon before him, Hitler found out that the Russian bear could not be taken. The German Forces began the long march back; it was only a matter of time now. In the city, the Germans turned on Jews as though they were to blame. Special squads entered ghetto and just shot anything and anybody they met. One day one of the members of this group was killed by a Jew; that very night, the Germans paid them back. They arrested all members of the Jewish police and forced them to the roof of the Jewish government building. With ropes tied around their necks, they told to jump off. Those who refused were kicked off, accompanied by the screams of the Jews and locals who watched this spectacle with equal horror.

Meanwhile, the Ukrainian Police rounded up about thirty Jews, lined them up against the wall and shot them down with machine pistols. The Germans and Ukrainians both looked drunk; they had to be to take part in such bestial thing. They kept shooting into the bodies along the wall until they all stopped moving, and only moans of crying civilians could be heard. One of the policeman came up to us and motioned for us to get away from the fence, "the show is over" he kept saying repeatedly. Stefan and I went home crying. This was the first time I ever saw Stefan so worked up over the Jews. I had not realized that he too long changed his mind about Jews in general. To hate them or disliked them was one thing, but to kill them just because they were Jews, that was different. No one had the right to do this. "Those bastards will pay for this," he kept muttering under his breath, "they will pay for this; this cannot go unchecked," He was right. The underground struck back at the Germans. No one was safe on the streets after dark anymore. The assassins were looking for Germans. However, the Germans were not taking any chances; any civilian caught on the streets after curfew would be shot on the spot. The war was on.

CHAPTER TWENTY

German Occupation
Spring 1943

Russians actions added to all this confusion. During each bombing raid, they would parachute terrorists. During the daylight hours, they would scout the city looking for concentrations of military vehicles and various other targets for the bombers. During the night, when the bombers arrived, the terrorists would fire flares in the direction of selected targets. Bombers would follow flares and drop flares to illuminate the area and follow up with bombs. This infuriated the Germans, and shot at anyone that moved during an air raid, not wanting to take any chances.

One night, couple of terrorists were cornered by the Germans in the house across the street. All night long and around noon the next day they held off the The German onslaught. Finally, the Germans, a tank was brought in and fired several rounds at the door. The return fire from the house had been sporadic for the past several hours and apparently, the terrorists were out of ammunition. Finally, following the tank, came the SS men. Slowly, they approached the hole in the door, their machine pistols held at ready. One after another they disappeared in the doorway. Suddenly, gunfire erupted viciously from the stairway. SS men froze in their tracks, several of them down on the ground, wounded or dead. They. Answered with their machine pistols, firing upstairs at the unseen enemy. Several hand grenades were tossed up the stairway. Slowly SS men resumed their forward progress. Then suddenly, two shots pierced the silence. One again the SS men stopped, anticipating a shower of bullets. But nothing happened, and the silence that followed told the story with eloquence that words could not explain. The terrorists had taken their own lives rather than face capture by the Germans.

Stefan and I had been standing along the house for hours, listening to all commotion and wondering what was going to happen. We saw them bring out the bodies. They seemed very young, in their early twenties, contingent was dismissed, leaving a guard around the building. The Gestapo would be back to investigate and try to determine why this particular house was chosen by the terrorists. I didn't envy the people living in that house.

Several days later, it was Sunday and was my turn to serve as altar boy at ten o'clock high mass. Everything went fine until about the end. Suddenly the anti-aircraft guns opened fire and the sound of falling bombs filled the air. I panicked, and quickly looked Father Roch who was saying the mass; He was completely unperturbed, as though he didn't a sound.

I looked around at the people in church; most of them were praying and occasionally, when a bomb would fall close by, their shoulders would shake. I was glad that the Mass was about over; I felt that there other much safer places to be at this time. Finally, when the last person at the communion rail was served, I uttered sigh of relief when we arrived at the sacristy. Father Roch didn't say anything; he just placed his hand on my head and patted me gently. "Don't be afraid boy," he said, "God is with us." Before I ad chance to answer, the sirens sounded all clear. The raid was over.

Later that morning, I found Father Leon and asked him how he felt during the raids. I asked him if he was afraid. "Yes, I am very afraid," he answered. "I go to the cellar every time somebody fires a shot around here," he said. "But why Father? You 'll go to heaven. So why worry?" He just looked at me. "Remember, God gave you your life, and it is your duty to protect it. You have no right to endanger it and this possibly will shorten your stay on this earth. As for me, I'm but a human being with many faults. I pray and hope that God will forgive me for my sins; yet I am very much afraid of dying right now. Not that I don't have faith in God. When He wants me to go, I will go. But I will not do anything that might unnecessarily endanger my life." I thanked him warmly. He was such a fine person; very understanding and very human. He understood my reason for asking and gave the reassurance he knew I needed.

CHAPTER TWENTY-ONE

German Occupation
Summer 1943

At the front, things were growing continually worse. The German Army was withdrawing all along the front and with each withdrawal, the actions against the Jews increased in ferocity. The ghettos were converted into slaughter houses. The action groups, both German and Ukrainians, would march in and shoot anyone in sight.

They were obsessed with the idea of mania that to destroy the Jews would stop the reverses at the front. It could not last much longer. The end for the Jews was near. It was summer now and the Russians were approaching the former Polish border in the east. For several days, the activity in the ghettos and concentration camps was on the raise. One could hear shooting all day long. The Germans didn't even bother to hide their activities any longer. Everyone knew that this was the end.

For days on end the trucks continued their shuttle between the stone quarry and the ghetto, each truck covered with tarpaulin, each with a guard sitting on the cab. In addition, some units of SS and Ukrainian Police continued their clean-up campaign in the ghetto which never stopped burning; there were dead bodies lying everywhere and the stench was beyond description. Still they continued, rounding up survivors and taking them on the last ride. This went on for several days, and then it stopped, as suddenly as it started.

Stefan and I walked slowly around the fence. The main gate was open now, with a single guard standing by. Around the fence were only few Ukrainian guards, looking bored and indifferent. We looked at the dead bodies lying in the streets, some already decomposing from the heat. Others were still intact, caught in escape or just peacefully lying there as though taking a sun bath; while still others were raising their arms in defense, or perhaps even in gesture of defiance or curse against the killers, their faces frozen with a deadly grin, their hungry bodies shrunken so that only skin and bones remained.

Slowly we continued, arriving finally at a small creek that flowed through the ghetto. We stopped with fright. The water was red with the blood of the victims. Slowly we crossed ourselves and said a quiet prayer. One could understand seeing all this death on the front lines, but these people were civilians, and their only crime was their religion. We couldn't go any further. We were both sick, before we could move again. That night, we relayed to our family what we had seen. No one said a word. Mother merely lowered her head, and I noticed that large tears were flowing down her cheeks. I suppose she was thinking about Mrs. Swartz, wondering if she were lying in the streets, or perhaps buried in the stone quarry. John too looked perplexed, his face very thoughtful. Suddenly, he banged the table with his fist and said fiercely: "and those bastards in London won't believe a single word of it when they receive my broadcast tonight. They just don't care. I hope that Janusz realizes this, I hope to hell he has forgotten his dream about a new and better Poland. Because these bastards in London don't want any changes. They want to return here after the war, claim all their former positions and powers, and return to the old status quo. Those sons of bitches are really suffering in the exile." Slowly his head bent down, and hide too began sob violently. "God, I hope that we know what we are doing," he kept whispering. "Don't let these poor kids do all this for nothing. They have forgotten how to live anymore. Don't let this to be in vain. God, give them a chance."

The next few days were horrible. We all felt depressed, knowing full well that within a very short time the Russians would be back. And then what? The German Army was continuing its withdrawal westward. It was understood that the city would not be defended. Several prominent buildings such as Post Office, the power plant, the railroad stations and several others were mined; the Germans weren't taking any chances.

Here the underground stepped in, they followed methodically the German Engineer troops, uncovering their wires to the various demolition targets and deactivated them. Others they would short out, making them more difficult to uncover. Our favorite trick was to push steel needle through a piece of wire, cutting it with the wire on both ends. This, I'm sure drove the Germans insane, for they could not detect the short without checking out the circuit every few feet. It was good to get few laughs at their expense for a change.

One afternoon I was summoned by Michael. There was to be an urgent meeting that evening and I was to be there at five PM sharp. By the time I arrived, the room was already filled with young boys. Quickly the unit commanders called the roll call. All were present. A sense urgency was prevalent. Slowly the curtain swung back and LT Andrew stepped in. I looked at him in amazement. Last time I saw him was about a month ago; he must have aged at least ten years during this time. His hair was now interlaced with gray. His face was haggard, and his eyes were deeply sunk. His voice seemed quieter.

"Gentlemen, we know the situation. It will be a matter of weeks before the Russians arrive. I don't need to remind you that we will continue fighting the Germans now, and when the Russians arrive, we will continue our struggle against them. We are still and always will be for a free Ukraine. Most of you probably have seen the traffic created by the shift of front lines. Our streets are crowded with heavy trucks, laden with supplies for the front. They must not reach their destination. This is our job. I want to see all unit commanders in my room for few minutes, rest of you stand by for orders."

We looked at each other. This was graduation for us, this we knew. No longer would we do the petty stuff. This time we would mean business. Shortly, the unit commanders returned and Michael advised his group that he would hold his meeting at our soccer field in one hour. "Don't stay in the open, but hide among the corn in the garden next to soccer field," he told us.

When I arrived there, I looked around. This was the first time that I could find out who my partners really were. It was a good feeling and I knew that they too felt the same way for I felt several of them staring at me. Michael was already there, and with him was an older member of the group. Quickly he started by saying that the meeting would now be turned over LT Jura, who was demolition expert. Without too much in the way of preliminaries, LT Jura proceeded with the instructions on fixing charges and their placement for maximum effect. These classes continued for three evenings. Finally, on the fourth evening LT Jura wished us luck and thanked us for our attention. He was returning to his unit. His job was done. Tonight, he would discover how well we had learned; tonight, we were to be given our first mission.

There were fourteen of us in this group, all between ages of fourteen and seventeen. Slowly Michael looked around us, he really looked happy and proud. "Gentlemen, we have our target for tonight. We will attack at midnight. I don't have tell you that it will be well past the curfew. You are on your own. We will split into groups of three, our target is the area between Green Street and Cherry Street. You may have noticed that the area is filled with large diesel trucks parked on both sides of the street. They are scheduled to leave tomorrow or they think they will be leaving." Here he smiled a little. "I hope that they are wrong," he said. Then proceeded to select the teams. By the time, he came to my name, there only three of us left, he, me and Stan, young boy of thirteen. "Well, I guess I'm lucky to have a protégé with me on this mission. We will take the corner of Green Street and Supinskiego Street. There is a garden. On the right side; I shall meet you under the large apple tree." We quietly shook hands and left. Michael would take care of explosives.

It was a long wait, and it really felt good when the time came for me to leave. Slowly I jumped the fence in the rear of our house. Darting from door to door I advanced toward the garden on Supinskiego street. So far so good. Quietly, I jumped over the fence and proceeded toward the apple tree. Michael was already there. Several minutes later our young friend Stan arrived. We were ready. Whispering, Michael outlined our plan of action. He and Stan would take the left side of the street, taking care of approximately seven trucks. I would handle the remaining three on the other side. Quietly he explained that the best way to knock out these trucks was to place explosives on top of the rear axle and don't make the fuse too long. He cautioned us to be careful to time them to allow plenty of time to place all charges. Then he asked us if we were ready. We nodded our heads and moved out towards our targets. Everything was quiet. It was extremely dark night as we moved from door to door, peering into the night, seeking enemy patrol. Suddenly Michael halted us. "After completing the job, continue on home. We will meet tomorrow and discuss the results." Again, we nodded our heads and proceeded toward the targets. Soon she was there.

Here we split. I stole across the street toward three large silhouettes parked at the curb. My heart was beating like a hammer. Slowly I crept from truck to truck placing the charges, expecting at any moment that I would feel the hand of the German soldier grabbing at me. But nothing happened. What seemed like an eternity took only very few minutes. I glanced at my watch, hoping that my explosives would not go off too soon. This would complicate things on the other side of the street. The last truck. Then I was on my way, being very careful not to be discovered. I headed across the field to get away from the target area and get home. I hadn't gone hundred yards when I heard rapid fire from machine pistol and several screams, followed by the sound of footsteps. Then the lights were turned on. Quickly I jumped to my feet and took off as if pursued by the devil. Then a deafening roar filled the air, mixed with screams of agony from the soldiers who had been sleeping in the trucks. Bedlam erupted behind me, everyone shouting and screaming. I didn't have much farther to go. Here was the fence; jump over, race upstairs, get into the house and crawl into bed. Mission completed - tomorrow we will get the results.

The next morning, I arrived at the school with great anticipation. On the way, there I had gone by the Green Street. Our job was accomplished 100 percent; most of the trucks were burned and while some had escaped, most of them were damaged beyond repair. It was a feeling of deep satisfaction that I felt. Our job was accomplished. In school, I looked for Michael but he was nowhere to be found. Finally, around noon, I located our young friend Stan. Quickly I asked him what happened. He merely shook his shoulders and said that the first several trucks had gone fine, but when they reached the last truck, there several German sleeping under the truck. By the time they realized this, it was too late; the Germans were awake and started to shout. He and Michael stood up and took off on dead run. Michael didn't make it, he was cut down by a machine pistol. I didn't hear rest of his words; everything went blank. I couldn't believe that Michael was dead. He was so young and such a good friend. I felt sick. The remainder of the day passed slowly as in a nightmare.

Once home I immediately went into my bedroom to seek little quiet. I don't know how long I lay there on the bed thinking about the activities of the previous night. Soon it grew dark and the sirens announced the arrival of the Russian planes. I didn't want to move. I was just tired and it really didn't matter anymore. I just stayed there in bed, not really being present there at all, my mind just wandering. When the air raid was over, everyone else came back upstairs to go to bed. Stefan didn't say a word when he found me in bed. He just asked me quietly to take my clothes off and go to sleep. During the next few days we remained very quiet. The Germans were going from house to house, searching and asking questions. They went through our apartment, we had a few tense moments, but it all proved to be a routine search. Finally, they gave up and left us alone.

CHAPTER TWENTY-TWO

German Occupation
Summer 1943

That day, coming from school, I met my fate. My friends and I were walking along the main thoroughfare, admiring the windows in "Nur fur Deutche" stores. When suddenly the Gestapo appeared, blocked off the streets and started to check the ID's. This was a routine procedure for them. Anyone caught without proper ID was evacuated to Germany on forced labor. They needed laborers in their war factories.

We merely laughed; this has happened before. We all had student ID's, and besides, we were much too young to be picked up for the labor force. Slowly the line advanced toward the check point. Some people were passed through, while others were told to get aboard the truck parked alongside the curb.

Finally, it was our turn. Confidently, we thrust our ID's at the German. He looked at them, looked back at us and motioned toward the truck. This was some kind of joke. We were students. We were children. This couldn't happen to us. Desperately, in

German, I tried to argue with him that he made some kind of error. Our student ID's were in order; we were students. He merely shrugged his shoulders and motioned toward the truck. This must be a mistake, I kept repeating to myself. They will let us go once we get to our destination, of this I was certain. Once I was settled in the truck, the reality of the imprisonment seemed to dawn on me. I tried to cling to the feeling that perhaps I would be released once we arrived at our destination, but then I wasn't too sure anymore.

I looked around at the truck full of people, some just laughing about the new situation, others morose, unsure of the future. There were only few boys of my age on the truck, and they all seemed as confused as me. We just weren't sure what the future had in store for us. Soon the tuck was full and we began to move. Slowly I watched the streets go by and then I realized our destination. We were going toward the prison. But this couldn't be - I really have not committed any crime! Could it be that they were aware of my association with the underground? No, that was absurd. They wouldn't catch me in the dragnet for that reason. I figured I would just wait and see what would happen.

It wasn't long before the truck stopped in front of a gate. There was some discussion in German and then truck proceeded through the gate. Behind us I heard the gate shut firmly; what an awful feeling; I thought. I felt like a bird in a cage; free, yet unable to go anywhere. Slowly we dismounted and were grouped together, awaiting orders from our captors. They made us form into a single line and march inside the building. Once in the building, we were forced to step in front of a desk, one at a time. There was Ukrainian Policeman behind a typewriter, methodically asking questions and preparing the forms committing us to the prison. He refused to answer any questions when asked, and occasionally he would lose his temper and scream at some poor soul into silence.

I still felt that there was some mistake, until my time came to register. Once that was completed and I still had not been released,

I knew that this was now a fact - I was going somewhere to help the German effort to win the war. How ridiculous, and yet, how lucky. I could have been registering in very much this fashion but under much worse circumstances. But now my registration was complete and I was given a number. I followed the guard into my cell. It was the fifth one in a long row. As I approached the door, several inmates looked me over very curiously, obviously amused and intrigued with my youth. The guard opened the door and motioned for me to enter. Before I realized what had happened, the heavy door slammed behind me and I was left to face my fellow inmates.

It was a very awkward moment. They were curious and somehow hostile, not trusting me perhaps, and anticipating some sort of treachery. Even in misery these people could not unite, always suspicious and anticipating the worse. Without a word, I walked to the center of the cell, looked around for a place to sit down, and walked over to the cots. There were only four of them, and there were ten of us. I sat down on the floor and placed my head between my knees, trying to figure out what had happened and what would come next. I wondered if Mother would be notified and what she could do to get me out of here. I was so engrossed in my thoughts that I was startled when a hand touched my shoulder and gentle voice said, "son who are you and why are you here?" I looked at an older face through my tears. I hadn't even realized that I was crying, but I was very lonely and very scared. Quietly I told him that I really didn't know why I was here; that there had been some sort of mistake and that I would probably be released tomorrow. We talked for a few minutes. It appeared that all the other inmates in the cell suffered the same calamity as me. They were all apprehended in a dragnet and now they were awaiting enough people to make up a transport. The was, of course, a rumor, but they felt certain that they would be going into Germany on forced labor. I had heard that the Germans were evacuating able bodied young men and women into Germany on forced labor to take the place of their own people who were being released for military service. Yes, but up to now they hadn't touched people of my age; we were much too young. Could to be possible that they had now changed their minds and had decided to take boys my age into forced labor? I hoped not. Yet it was true. Several days and nights went by and no one inquired of me why I was there. As a matter of fact, we were completely ignored by our captors except for the food and periodic name checking. At first I could not eat, but the old gentlemen who had befriended me, insisted that I eat something. "It will be a long journey, son," he kept saying. "You must preserve your strength."

Finally, time ceased to matter. I was hoping that we could get out of jail soon. I really didn't care anymore where we were going. I just wanted to get out into fresh air, and be able to move around without rubbing elbows with my fellow inmates every time I turned around. I lost all hope of seeming my family or getting a word out to them. I had approached our Ukrainian guard with the request, but he merely asked me how much I could pay for the favor. Unfortunately, I didn't have any money, and he didn't want to be bothered.

The rumor kept circulating that we would be going to Dachau, the infamous concentration camp outside Munich. But why? What had we done to deserve such a punishment? More rational rumors had us going somewhere in Germany to be assigned to some munition factory. Each day seemed to bring more young boys into the jail. A couple more were ushered to our cell just a few days later. They related that the authorities had decided that sixteen years old was old enough for the forced labor battalions and that they were being evacuated left and right. I sighed with relief, for, cruel as it seemed, I now felt certain that my family knew why I disappeared. It was something, anyway. Perhaps John and his superiors could do something for me, who knows?

A couple more days went by, and then around noon a guard opened our door and mentioned for us boys to come out. Quickly we shook hands all arounds us and wished each other well. We somehow knew that we would not be returning to the cell this time. Our hearts beating rapidly, we followed the guard. Soon were in the office, a long auditorium like room. It was crowded with boys about our age, and at the end of the room were eight field desks staffed by Ukrainian policemen. Over the loudspeakers, we were told to lineup in front of the tables. Once again, the long wait, the same monotonous questions, the same waiting. Several hours later, when all the preliminaries had been completed, once again the loudspeakers ordered us to line up in four singles files. The guards were all arounds now. It was getting dark outside. The yard was filled with trucks. We were ordered into the trucks, and then slowly the convoy began to move.

Soon we were in the city, moving rapidly now with an escort. We could not look out; the curtain was drawn tightly on the truck. After what seemed like eternity, the trucks came to a halt and the curtains were drawn back. We were ordered out. I looked around me. We were at a railroad siding; the entire area was surrounded by Ukrainian Police and Gestapo. They just weren't taking any chances. There were some civilians present there, too, just looking at us, wondering who we were and where we were being taken. Some of the people were visibly crying. Now the Germans are getting at the children; this is too much. Will they ever stop?

We didn't have time to wonder what was going to happen. We were ordered into the waiting box cars, forty men per car, and again the doors were shut behind us. Only once they were open again; this time some food was stuck into the car, and the door was shut once more. It was pitch dark. It wasn't too long, however, before the train began to move. Now the silence was broken with sobs; then everyone joined in. We felt so alone and so lost. We had no idea where we were going to be doing. We were so young. I suppose it showed, in the fact that no one was ashamed of his feelings. We all hoped that our families would know what happen to us and, most important of all, that we would see them again once this this whole mess was over.

Yet, I couldn't help but wonder if I would ever see my home again. Would I ever return there, or would I give my life somewhere in the strange land, fighting a strange war? Not really wanting to, but forced to because of my age and because Germany needed manpower. Strangely enough, I thought, most of us will probably die from bombs dropped by our supposed friends, England and America. Ironic, yet true.

Soon the monotonous rhythm of the wheels passing over the break in the rails relaxed me and I grew tired. I felt around me; the floor was covered with straw. Well, might as well get some sleep, I thought, who knows what the next few days will bring. Sometime during the night, we stopped and changed guards, apparently after crossing the border. A little later, just about daybreak, the door swung open and we greeted by corporal from Luftwaffe. Smiling, he said, "Meine Herren, good morgen; Wie gets es Ihnen?" Alarmed we looked at our new guest. What was going on? Slowly I approached the soldier and asked him, "wohin gehen wir?" "Langsam, langsam", he replied smilingly. "Nicht so schnell." We all crowded around the door. It was nice to smell fresh air and be able to look out and the light. We were at some siding, apparently waiting for some train to pass us. Meanwhile, some Luftwaffe soldiers came over and soon they brought some food and asked us to eat and relax. This was pleasant change. We ate heartily and joked with the soldiers.

I sat next to the corporal and kept asking him about future. But he merely laughed and told me not to worry, saying we were not the property of the Luftwaffe but they look after us. He told us that in just few more hours we would reach our destination. There we would be given a bath and new clothing, and it would be explained what was to be expected of us. Haltingly, we asked if it would be all right for us to leave the door open while the train was in. Motion.

"Sicher," he replied. "I will be your companion in the car until we reach your destination." OH boy, what a relief. At least we would be able to watch the countryside and see where we were going. The excitement of the trip was reaching its climax and home and the life we had known were now far behind us. A new future was ahead and with it, new adventure. It really was getting quite exciting now. I looked around me, apparently, I wasn't the only one who felt like this. All around me I saw young faces, eager to see the world and somehow confident that they would see it through and manage to enjoy life regardless of what the future would bring.

Soon the train began moving again. It was different now. The door was wide open, a bar placed across the open space to prevent anyone of us falling out. Our Luftwaffe friend was sitting next to the door, enjoying the trip as much as we were. We waved at people in the fields, and they waved back, not knowing who we were, probably not caring. Around four in the afternoon we approached a small town. I managed to read the sign, OPPELN. Here the train stopped and again we were told to remain in the cars until told to unload.

The railroad yard was full of trucks, with Luftwaffe and SS men everywhere. And yet, it was different atmosphere than at home; they seemed relaxed and really lost human. Of course, they had a job to do and I didn't doubt at all that they would at any one waiting to escape. But then, why should we escape? We didn't even know where we were or what we would be doing. One by one the by the box cars were emptied and the boys were getting on the trucks. Then it was our turn. "Auf wiedersehen" shouted our Luftwaffe friend. "Auf wiedersehen sehr schenell" I shouted back at him, I noticed that he smiled.

CHAPTER TWENTY-THREE

German Occupation
Summer 1943

Then our truck was moving down the road. In about ten minutes we had passed the town and were now on the open road. This time the truck was open and we looked around curiously, wondering where we were. It wasn't too long before we stopped in front of a gate. The ramp swung upward, and we proceeded into the compound. It was a Kaserne. As soon as the truck stopped, we were told to dismount and stay in a group. Everyone remained on the parade ground with several SS men milling around, talking and joking. When the last truck arrived, we were told to gather around a stand that stood in the center of the field. What appeared to be colonel in the SS mounted the steps, surrounded by some Luftwaffe officers and noncommissioned officers. A tall Hitler Jungend followed them to the stand. We were curious now, wondering what would happen next. Soon the loudspeaker crackled and came to life. The SS man was speaking.

"Meine Herren, Ich grüße euch in Deutschland." The tall Hitler Jungend translated the speech in Ukrainian. It wasn't very long speech; he merely told us that we were in Oppeln, in the Sudetenland. We would be here for two months, during which time we would train in the art of marching and other military discipline. As soon as he said this, I said to myself; so that's what it is. For past, several months the Germans had been recruiting young boys for the auxiliaries in the Luftwaffe. Posters proclaimed many advantages of joining up, such as good food, travel, and a place in the Neues Europa, a term that was being repeated over and over again. Yes, Neues Europa alright; all for the Germans and nothing for us. But apparently, there weren't many takers so now the authorities had decided to try a different means. We were conscripted whether we liked or not. So, we would do our part for the Neues Europa and dodge bullets of our friends, the Allies. It was a crazy war.

The Colonel continued: "You will receive adequate training and maintenance here. You will be treated like any soldier. If you do well and learn quickly you will be rewarded; on the other hand, if you don't, you will be punished. Your cadre will consist of men from the Luftwaffe and the Hitler Jugend. Some of your own people who show leadership qualities will be promoted so you may have your own leadership. But I cannot impress upon you too strongly the fact that the Reich is at war. You are now a member of the force that is fighting for the Neues Europa - that term against. You must do your part or you will be punished as a traitor. We will do all we can to make your stay here comfortable." Here he stopped. He raised his arm high and shouted, "Heil Hitler!" His entourage followed and replied, "Heil Hitler." The speech was over. The Colonel stepped down from the stand, followed by his cohorts. Only the noncommissioned officers remained.

The Hitler Jugend asked for a show of hands for those among us who spoke and understood German. I raised my hand along with several others. By this time my German wasn't bad at all. Quickly we were segregated, while the others were being divided into groups of fifteen or more, while were approached by the Sargent Major of the Luftwaffe. He seemed to be approximately forty-five years old and mean. He surveyed our group and spoke in broken Polish. "A wy skund jestescie?" We were shocked. What is going on? If they spoke Polish, why ask if we spoke German? What are they trying to do, warn us not to try anything fancy? "Lemberg" she replied in unison. "Oh yes, Lemberg, the beautiful old city. I was there for about a year in the hospital, recovering from wounds received on the Easter Front." "I hope that you will feel at home at this camp. The food is good; you will work hard and before long you will depart to do your share in the war. I can't tell you where you will end up, for I don't this myself. But I don't worry about it. While you are here, you will be in my charge; I will be your Father Confessor.

"I might as well tell you right now that I'm a no-good-son-of-a-bitch. I will work your asses off and I will not put up with any gold bricking. You people will help me. You all speak German, or so you said. We will see. You will each be assigned to a group of boys, possibly one person per room. You will be in charge. Tomorrow morning the others will be told this. You will establish a link between them and us. This is necessary, for you are young and have a lot to learn.

You must play ball with us; you have no other choice. If you don't, there are other places that we can send young I don't believe that I have to explain." No, he didn't; we knew perfectly well what he meant. "The first thing I want you to establish yourself. In some cases, it will not be easy. But you must have their confidence. I am not going to tell how to do it. I will hold you responsible for anything or anybody who has been entrusted to you. You must work with us and with them. Again, it won't be easy. Don't expect any special favors, for you won't get them. You will be judged harder than the rest, for you should know better; you are all intelligent; you speak our language and therefore there will be no excuse for you. You must do as you are told and you make sure the communications get to the last man in your room. Are there any questions?"

Yes, there were thousands of questions, but how do you ask them? How do you ask a man who just told you that you are on your own? You must make the first move yourself. But how? Yes, we are all from the same area, southeast Poland, but here the similarity ends. I hardly knew them, and as luck would have, my physical make up certainly didn't convey any fear or command respect. I was probably the smallest of the whole bunch.

One by one we introduced ourselves to the Sergeant Major. He shook our hands and assigned a room to each of us. When my turn came, I noticed a smile in his eyes and I guessed that he was wondering how I was going to manage to control my group. "Junge," he said, "wo bist du here?" "Lemberg, Herr....."Schneider." He filled in the name for me. His hand slapped me on the back and added quickly, "Good luck," and walked away. Yes, good luck. Brother, am I ever going to need it.

Slowly I walked toward the building. My room was on the second floor, room number eight. I stopped by the door, took a deep breath and walked in. As soon as I walked in I heard someone shout "Achtung." Everyone in the room jumped to his feet. Alarmed, I looked around. Beside the first double bunk I noticed our friend from the train. Apparently, he had been busy in the room while I was getting the briefing from Sergeant Schneider. "Reart euch," I replied, and turned toward my friend. He came forward with his hand out stretched. I grasped it firmly.

"My name is Kurt", he said. He led me toward my bunk; he had somebody fix it for me. All the time he kept talking to me, and meanwhile, my comrades kept a respectful silence and distance. He told me that he was assigned to this room and that anything I wanted would have to go through him. However, he felt that certain that we would enjoy our stay here. He felt that we had a good bunch here and they would not present any problems. He said that with little of time they would become good workers. He cautioned me that lights had to be out at 10 pm and there would be no talking thereafter. Once the lights were off it was time for rest. I glanced at my watch, fifteen more minutes.

Slowly I returned to the center of the room. Calmly, or at least pretending that I was calm, I introduced myself. I told them that I was room chief, that any problems they had would have to go through me. I was their liaison with the authorities. I tried to indicate that I was one of them, but somehow, I felt that I didn't come across too well. I sensed resentment in some that one of them that one of them has already turned against them and tried to order them around. Of course, I expected this, for wasn't it too difficult to understand. After all, we should remember when our own Police was worse than the Gestapo and the SS? Yes, I felt certain that they were. And so, the same applied here. It would take some time, and meanwhile I had no choice but to insist that they should do as I told them. The big test would come tonight after the lights were out, and this was certain.

After my brief speech, I returned to my bunk. I must have looked worried, for Kurt patted me on the shoulder and said not to worry. Everything is going to be alright. I smiled weakly; sure, everything is going to be prima. I lay down on the bunk, looking around me, taking in everything around me. This is what I will be living with for God knows how long; better get acquainted with.

The room was fairly large, permanent building, everything nice and clean. Down along each wall stood a row of double bunks, forty to fifty men in the room. God, and they are all my responsibility. How am I going to handle them? I don't even know most of them. But this was my problem. Suddenly I wished I had kept my mouth shut rather than volunteering information about my knowledge of German. Well, it was too late now. The decision was made for me. I was expected to handle the situation. And yet, perhaps I could help them, speak for them when it became necessary. After all, they couldn't defend themselves; they couldn't speak the language. Perhaps it was my duty to speak up when I did.

It wasn't too long before the lights were turned off. At first there was considerable noise, with everyone getting accustomed to this new life. But soon the trip took its toll and the conversations died down as everyone settled down to sleep, hoping that the dawn would bring a good day. I couldn't sleep. The events of the past several days were still fresh in my mind. I couldn't help but wonder what my family was doing. Did they know that I have been caught by the Germans and taken into Germany to join the Luftwaffe? Would we be able to communicate with them? I was wondering about my underground unit, too; would I be missed? Would they continue to carry on even after the Germans left the city? How would the Russians act once they recaptured Lwow? I was certain that they would be back. I felt certain, too, that the Germans had already lost the war and that it was only a matter of time before it became obvious to all. Soon I too became tired, and before I knew it, I was sound asleep.

CHAPTER TWENTY-FOUR

Oppeln Sudetenland
Summer 1943

The next morning, we were awakened early. Quickly we were ordered to get up, clean up and get ready for breakfast. Immediately following breakfast, we were marched over to the supply room to draw our uniforms. It was quite a mess. Nothing fit properly, but no matter, it was a pleasant change. Immediately following this, we were again assembled on the parade ground and the same colonel again mounted the platform. As on the day before, he was surrounded by officers and NCO's from the SS and Luftwaffe. Sergeant Schneider called us to attention, saluted the colonel and gave us "At ease."

The same Hitler Jugend acted as an interpreter. This time the speech was little longer. We finally found out what we were expected to do and where we would eventually go. "Gentlemen, you have spent your first night in this camp. As you have no doubt observed, this is a military camp. You have been entrusted to the care of Luftwaffe. You have noticed, I'm sure, that your uniforms are blue in color, after the Luftwaffe. Your principal reason for being here is to train as soldiers. You will be taught basic military courtesy and dismounted drill. Upon graduation from here, you will be assigned to various units throughout Germany. You will be assigned to Luftwaffe Communication Battalion. There are several different groups within this Battalion and you will be assigned to them based on your skills. Needless to say, you are now under military jurisdiction any crimes committed by you subject to Military Court.

"You have no doubt met your cadre." Here other members of the cadre were introduced. "Sergeant Schneider will be your immediate Commander. Listen to him well; he is an old and dedicated soldier. He will work you hard but you can learn a lot from him. In addition, each platoon has one of your own people as translators. They are there to help you and you must obey them as you would one of the cadre. They will act as link between you and us." Here he stopped. "Heil Hitler" he shouted. The assembly again answered in unison, "Heil Hitler." He turned around, descended from the platform and left.

Now we were introduced to our cadre. Quickly we were broken into platoons. My good fortune prevailed; Kurt stayed with me as a cadre. He called a meeting. I felt very important since this was my first official duty. Slowly Kurt explained to our group what was expected of us. I translated for him, sentence after sentence, trying to make it sound impressive. Kurt made sure that they understood that this was a serious business. In a way, we had a good deal; we weren't going to work in factories. We had a chance to fight in battle for the Neues Europa. He made sure that they understood that any problems would have to be cleared through me, and by same token, I was left completely in charge of them in the absence of the cadre. The stay here would be fairly short, about two and half months; then we would graduate and depart for various assignments.

And so, the time went by, quickly at first, and then more slowly as we got used to the monotony of our existence. There was nothing to do in the evenings; we were not allowed to leave compound and naturally, we were very lonely and tired. The routine that had been quite interesting at first soon became very boring. We got up early and went for half hour of physical training, which consisted of several exercises and a short run. After this, we returned to the barracks to wash and clean up. After breakfast, we went to our classes. At first, we were being taught on parade ground. As soon as we became proficient in marching, we marched out into the city to train on local sports fields. This was lot of fun, for we always managed to create a show when we came marching down the street, always proudly trying to keep in step and singing marching songs.

It really was nice to see so many people line up along the streets and wave marveling that boys of our age could perform so well. Of course, there were many young girls on the streets too, and this was always a welcome sight. Our marches became longer in duration, and always, during the march, we would invariably have heard the command, "Enemy aircraft overhead." Immediately we would disperse, jumping into ditches on both sides of the road. Then we would reassemble, march for a while, and repeat the process. I suppose they were trying to get us get used to the idea that the planes, enemy planes, would be our constant companions in the near future.

During the breaks, Kurt and I talked a great deal. He was a very pleasant fellow and I grew fond of him. He told me that he was from a small village in Austria. One of three brothers, he was the only one left, the other two were killed on the eastern front. The only reason he was here with us was that he was recuperating from wounds also received on the eastern front. He was about twenty-two years old. In many ways, a wise man having gone through hell; he spoke of the Russians with such a viciousness that I thought him to be sick. I suppose he had the right to feel this way, but on the other hand, who did declare the war?

Often, we would continue our discussions in the evenings. He was curious about conditions in Poland before the war, wondering how the people lived. This always reminded me of my discussions with my Russian friend's father. However, this time it was different; Kurt was genuinely interested and was closer to my age. I told him about our life, the war, and the actions taken by my father. I told him about the occupation by the Russians and the terrible persecutions. Then came the German occupation, and without any hesitation, I told him of my feelings about the Gestapo and the SS men who had carried out such atrocities against the Jews.

Here he became extremely angry and nervous. He told me that he personally hated the SS; that they were animals, dedicated to the principle that could not possibly work. He told me about the conditions on the front lines, where the SS men would shoot at the Werhmacht soldiers if they decided to abandon positions in the face of superior Russian forces. He told me that the average German wished that the war sere over so that they could return to living a normal life. He indicated that he felt that Germany had lost the war, but was hanging on merely because Hitler would not give up. He talked about the bombings of major German cities, decrying the necessity for such a slaughter.

Sometimes we would sit in silence for a long time, just listening to boys singing about our home town, always so sad and helpless. I realized then that our chances of ever returning home were indeed slim. Kurt explained to me that the reasons for having us under the auspices of Luftwaffe rather than SS was humanitarian. Should we decide to make a break for it, and should we be apprehended by the Russians, our chances of living through such an ordeal were rather dubious. I remember hearing stories about prisoners from the SS Galicia, a SS Division made of Ukrainian volunteers from my region who fought on the side of Germans, but only against the Russians. Anyone caught as a prisoner could expect to be shot on the spot, or hung immediately from the nearest lamp post or a tree.

It took me a while to get used to the idea that there was no mother to take care of my things; that unless I do my own washing, I would have to go around in dirty clothing. It was quite an education, but soon I got used to the idea and became accustomed to the new routine. This was quite strange period for us. We were at war; and yet to us war seemed quite remote. Rarely did we see Allied bombers. We did get air raid warnings, but the plains were only silver spots high in the sky, completely oblivious of our existence, intent on flying in the direction of Germany.

Our homeland being invaded for the second time by the Russians, and the Germans were losing the war. And yet, all around us we saw signs of confidence that Germany would eventually win the struggle. All this time, Hitler kept talking about his new "secret weapon." Then finally, our training was over; one more week to go and we will depart from here. I was somehow sad. I had grown to like and enjoy this peaceful camp in the Sudeten. I had become very fond of Kurt and somehow felt that I would suffer a terrible personal loss by leaving him.

CHAPTER TWENTY-FIVE

Oppeln Sudetenland
Summer 1943

Many nights, after our discussions, I would lie awake trying to think out the problems we were faced with. How could I possibly hate the Germans for what they had done in Poland? I couldn't possibly blame the entire nation for the crimes of the few and yet, didn't the people know what was going on in the concentration camps? Why didn't they do something about it? I was never able to make my mind up fully as to how I felt. I suppose in the final analysis I realized that some of the were ignorant or just didn't want to the miserable truth that they were living with. Perhaps it was better that way; just live your own life and forget what is going on around you. This was too confusing and too complex for me. Someday perhaps I would find an answer to all of this.

And then the day arrived; today was our graduation. At high noon we marched onto the parade ground and faced parade platform. It was all decorated with Luftwaffe flags; several dignitaries were milling around the stand. Immediately in front of the stand, the Hitler Jugend were assembled there with their flags and drum and bugle corps; we were called to attention. Then slowly and majestically the notes of "Deutchland uber alles" filled the air. Hitler Jugend Honor Guard executed "present arms" and the last notes sounded, we were given "at ease." The SS Colonel came to the mike and congratulated us for working hard for the Neues Europa. The speeches from various dignitaries continued with the same messages about Neues Europa. After the speeches, we marched back to the Kaserne for the last time. We were given the rest of the day to get ready for tomorrows departure.

I stayed in my bunk, oblivious to what was going on. I was really confused now. I hated to see those boys leave. I have grown so fond of them. We had had a few problems but they had worked out all right. I was wondering where I would end up next. I hated the war at that moment with all my passion. I had been through this before. Get to know somebody, become fond of him, and he would disappear from my life as sure as the sun would rise again tomorrow. I was sick of it. My thoughts went back to Janusz and I wondered how he was doing. Did he ever get his wish to see his Polish Government in exile really interested in a new Poland, or was he disappointed, too, and frustrated with the outcome of the war?

I thought of John and Stefan, hoping that they were all right. Mother and Anna needed them around the house. I shuddered at the thought that the too might have been caught and sent someplace into Germany on forced labor. What would Mother and Anne do alone with two small children? Quickly I forced myself to turn to other things.

I got up and went out to take a walk. The parade ground was full of people; some were laughing, others were just hanging around in small groups, sad because of their impending departure and the possibility of separation. As the evening approached, there came the inevitable songs of home. This time, however, they sounded much sadder and hopeless. I joined the group around the steps.

They were quiet, talking about the "good old days" at home; reliving some funny incidents in their lives, talking about our home town, Lwow, with affection as though talking about their girls. Yes, it was a beautiful city, old, but beautiful. So, full of laughter and happiness. Then they grew quiet and one boy started to sing solo a song about our city. Soon was joined in the refrain by the rest the boys and it wasn't long before we were all sobbing like little children, which, I know now, she really was.

Sleep was hard to come that night. For long while I tossed in my bunk, trying to clear my mind of many thoughts, hoping just to relax and close my eyes and sleep. I heard someone walking softly towards my bunk and as I looked up I saw Kurt, dressed in trousers, t-shirt and sandals. He sat on the edge of my bunk and slightly touched my hand. "George, I'm going to miss you," he whispered softly. "I have grown very fond of you." Tears came to my eyes as I to return the squeeze of his hand and admit that too regretted my departure. "However," he added, "You will be all right." Five of you German speaking boys will be assigned to Lufwaffe Construction Company now being formed. You will enjoy the work, and I feel certain that you will prefer this to working in some munition factory. At least you will travel a lot and see the world. It will be hard manual work, but your group will fairly small, thus it shouldn't be too bad." Then he fell silent. After a while, he started talking very softly. "We have had many talks together. He has expressed views for which, if exposed, both of us could have been punished very severely. Yet, there we were, placed together by the fortunes of war. You have trusted me and I had complete confidence in you. I have learned much from those discussions and I only hope that I have managed to convey to you the awful circumstances which surround us, the German nation." "I know that you have often wondered how we could close our eyes to what is going on in the concentration camps and just lead lives. Remember, there isn't a single family in Germany today doesn't have some member either dead, wounded or missing at the front, or have someone close in one of the services. You ask how a soldier, be he SS or regular infantry, can kill innocent civilians just because there is a war going on? I cannot offer you the answer. I have often wondered after our conversations what would happen if I were presented with such a situation. I feel certain now that I would refuse such an order regardless of the outcome. I realize now that the excuse that we had to follow the orders or suffer ourselves is no longer adequate. George, try to understand us. We suffered a great deal in the immediate post World War I years. During the twenties, the economic conditions were beyond description. Then came Hitler and promised us something - the dignity to be a German. And he wiped out the shame of the Versailles. We were blind to the outcome of the plans laid down by this mad man. We were living in a dream, hoping to get all the benefits with the minimum of sacrifices on our part. Well, were mistaken if we thought that we could get away with it. We are now paying the price, and once this conflict is over, Germany will be shamed for years to come. However, George, you seen much in life already. I have feeling that you have not told me everything. It doesn't matter; some things are best left unsaid. But you must have compassion for us. Yours is the generation that is now growing up, living the times. Look around you. You cannot indiscriminately blame every German for the crimes committed by the few. If you do, you will know better than they. Remember this." He was overcome with emotion. Again, he squeezed my had. "Auf wiedersehen, machs good junge," he whispered. Then he walked out.

Next morning, we got up early. There was so much packing to do to get ready for our departure. The final formation was set for 8 am on the parade ground. Once again, the colonel mounted the platform, but this time his speech was very brief. He thanked us for our cooperation and for getting the job done. He wished luck and a safe journey. Immediately, Sergeant Schneider told. Everyone to sit down. Then his Administrator began reading a long list of names. Everyone called was ordered to pick up his baggage and moved out. The trucks were getting ready. Hours went by. Finally, there only few of us left.

CHAPTER TWENTY-SIX

Assignment Bavaria
Fall 1943

Five names were called - Fuchs, Yarbor, Olijnik, Trud and me. We were told to report to Sergeant Major's office. Once there, Sergeant Schneider told us what had already been told me by Kurt the previous night. We were to proceed by train to a small village in Bavaria. There we were to join a Luftwaffe Telegraph Construction Company which had just lost all its German soldiers to front line duty in the East. The Company was just being converted into Luftwaffe Auxiliaries from Belarus and Western Ukraine. The need for German speakers from southeast Poland to work with Cadre there to aid them in conducting training in construction of telegraph lines. This sounded very exciting. I looked my friends over; Fuchs and Olijnik I knew from school; the other two I have seen around the compound. Sergeant Schneider introduced us and as parting remark, added; "You boys have it made. Now just don't screw up. Play it by ear. You deserve the break you have gotten. You worked hard for me and you did damn good job.

The rest is up to you. Sergeant Schoen will accompany you to your destination."

Immediately after dinner, we loaded our gear on truck and departed for the train station. The trip was very enjoyable. It was the first time in my life that I took such a long journey. It took us about twelve hours to get to our destination; almost all night I stood at the window watching the scene around me. By the next morning, I was dead tired but thrilled with the thought of a new experience. The adventure of it was very appealing to me.

Sergeant Schoen was very nice fellow. He didn't bother us the whole trip. He was handling all necessary arrangements, and he told when to us change trains, what to do, and where to go. We were glad that he came along. People were curious about our youth and our foreign talk, and he gladly supplied the answers to the many questions about us.

Finally, we arrived at our destination, where we were met by a truck at the station. We were expected; that was something. After very short ride, we stopped in front of a school building. We dismounted and looked about us curiously. It was a very small village, and a small gathering of local children greeted us silently. They were staring at us, not knowing what to make of us. The driver of the truck told us to go in and report to the commander.

We followed Sergeant Schoen into the office that once belonged to the principle of the school. There we were met by an Oberfeldfebel from the Luftwaffe. He looked big and ugly. His name was Heinrich Stutz, and I hated him from the very first moment that I laid my eyes on him. He listened to Sergeant Schoen's report, and then addressed us in broken Polish. "Siadajcie, chce zwami pogadac." We complied with his request and sat around the table. For a few seconds, he just looked us over. Then he started speaking, this time in German.

"I want you to know that I didn't ask for you. The people above me decided that your kind was necessary for our operation so you were selected. I have read your reports about your performance in the training camp in Oppeln. You guys seemed to be some kind hot shots. Well, you will have prove it to me. As far as I'm concerned, you're just bunch of damn foreigners. You'll do as you're told, and you will cooperate with us in getting the message over to your compatriots. I will not put with any nonsense. If I see any sign of disobedience, you'll be destroyed. Am I making myself clear?" Yes, you fat slob, I thought to myself. You're making yourself clear. I will and stay away from you as much as I can.

He turned to one of his assistants and asked to get the remainder of the contingent. As it turned out, there only eight Germans assigned to this group. Two of them were truck drivers, two cooks, and the rest our cadre. One by one we were introduced. One of the drivers was very young and the other was much older, much quieter and somewhat aloof. The three-cadre other than Stutz, were of middle age. There was Obergefreiter Schmidt, Unteroffizier Rice and Unteroffizier Klein, the last looking like a pig, and, since he spoke Polish, apparently raised in the Silesian Region.

"Gentlemen, these five boys are here to aid you and assist you in conducting your training. I have explained to them what is expected of them. Are any questions?" There were none, so we were dismissed. Unteroffizier Rice took us upstairs to our quarters, one small classroom converted into barracks. Our beds consisted of some straw covered by a blanket. This was the extent of our furnishings. We unloaded our baggage and sat down to discuss the situation. Fuchs was the first to explode. "That son of a bitch. Who the hell he thinks he is, anyway?" We were pretty much put out by our greeting, but what else could we expect? After all, we were forced into this, so we might as well grin and bear it.

The remainder of the day was spent on meeting the company and discussing future plans. There were approximately sixty men in the company. They all came from White Russia and greater Ukraine. They distrusted us from the start, I suppose, if we were dupes of the Germans. Fuchs became our spokesman, since he was the oldest and cocky. That night, after supper, he called a meeting. This of course, had to be cleared with Sergeant Stutz, who immediately ordered Sergeant Kline to monitor it.

Fuchs introduced us one by one. He told them how we found ourselves in this situation we were in and told them our training in Oppeln and our subsequent assignment here. In addition, he told them what we knew about the next few weeks with this group. Still, there were no questions. They looked at us with hostility. We made two mistakes. We were from Galicia; thus, as far as they were concerned, we were Polish Ukrainians, and secondly, we spoke German; thus, we were not to be trusted.

The following day a formation was called. The Company Commander wished to welcome us to the unit. As we assembled in the yard, Sergeant Stutz called the group to attention and reported to the Captain in the Luftwaffe. He wore pilot's wings on his chest and I wondered what he is doing here, until I noticed that his right hand was very stiff and covered with a brown leather glove. His right arm had been amputated. His name was Captain Kluge. He asked for volunteer from us to assist him in his speech and as always, Fuchs volunteered. Captain Kluge was excellent speaker, a man who believed in his duty and who was determined to get the job accomplished; obviously, a devout NAZI. He welcomed us to the unit and told us what to be expected of us. He talked about the importance of communication in modern warfare and finally he told us that we were fortuned to have a part in helping the Third Reich in rebuilding Europe in the new image. With this he was finished. Lieutenant Gluck was left behind to supervise the training.

CHAPTER TWENTY-SEVEN

Training
Fall 1943

For the first week, we had classes all day long dealing mainly with the various tools employed by a telegraph building company in accomplishing its tasks. They were very interesting and very exhausting; it was extremely difficult to translate many of the terms and it took a considerable amount of time to get accustomed to this sort of thing. During the second week, we went out into the field and cut down the trees for the poles; dug holes, and set the poles into the holes. Later these used for instruction and practice on how to climb the posts with the half-moon shape climbers. I really enjoyed the climbing part of the training and became quite adept at this art. It really was a lot of fun for the youngsters.

One afternoon, upon returning from the training site, we found the doors to the closed. Sergeant Stutz informed us that we would be permitted to enter the building five at a time only to pick up our rucksacks and report immediately for inspection for any unauthorized equipment. I panicked, for the five of us knew that Yarbor had a P-38 pistol. We knew, too, that if they ever found this out, we all would be dead. Yarbor went first, and I was held up for the second group. I often wonder how in the hell he could get the pistol out of rucksack and stick it into his pocket on the way to the inspection lane and pass the pistol to me. Sergeant Kline noticed my moving about and ordered me to do ten deep-bends. Each time I did one of them, I wondered if the pistol was going to fall out from my pocket. Fortunately for all of us, it didn't. When the time came for me to be inspected, I passed the pistol to Fuchs. By doing so, we could outfox our friends. However, we had our warning. In the future, we will be more careful. The inspection revealed only that some people had too much underwear which they had to give up. Nothing more serious happened.

One good thing about this assignment was that we were completely free to move about. Of course, we didn't have any money so were unable to buy anything. Yet, the freedom was a good feeling. In the evenings, we took a stroll around the village, talking to the locals. They were very pleasant, always so glad to hear us converse with them in their native tongue. And so, a couple of weeks went by. More training and more work.

One evening, our supper meal was extremely bad. It consisted of meat and potatoes, but the potatoes been frozen and had a sickly taste. We boycotted the kitchen and refused to eat. We demanded to see and speak with Lieutenant Gluck. Unfortunately, he was visiting Headquarters and the only person we could speak was Sergeant Stutz. This of course, was waste of time. He was enraged at our behavior. He cursed until foam formed at the corners of his mouth. He threatened us court martial and many other forms of punishment. Still we refused to eat. It seems that one of the boys assigned to kitchen had noticed that the cadre had fresh potatoes while we were given the rotten frozen ones. Since neither side would compromise, we were restricted to the building that night.

The next morning, while the rest of the company was training on the poles, we five were ordered to report to the office. Lieutenant Gluck was present at this time. Again, Fuchs related the story to the Lieutenant about the food situation. He listened very quietly, and Fuchs was through, he asked us if we thought we had behaved properly. We answered that we had grievances which we presented to Sergeant Stutz who completely ignored them. I don't know how we got away without being punished. The food did improve, temporarily anyway, and everything seemed to go well for a while. Except for one thing. We knew that we had an enemy, whom we couldn't trust, and who would destroy us at the first opportunity. "That son of a bitch is dead if he keeps messing with me, Fuchs snapped angrily." This was getting serious, and we decided to lie low for a while. We were having good time, why mess it up?

That night Fuchs and I went out to see the town. After strolling aimlessly for couple of hours, we found a bench and sat down. Before long, the bench next to us was occupied by two young girls. This was all that Fuchs needed, and before I realized what was going on, we were sitting with the girls and Fuchs was telling a fantastic tale about us, and about the unit. The girls were sisters. Fuchs was with Helen and I with Anita, her younger sister. I was extremely bashful and scared, not knowing what to do. At Fuchs suggestion, we took a walk around the park. Occasionally, I would steel a glance at him and he was having a great time, his arm around Helen's waist, and she was obviously enjoying the fun. Casually, I reached for Anita's hand. Even in the darkness, I knew that her face turned crimson. We talked for a while, complete oblivious to our surroundings, and when I looked up, Fuchs and Helen were gone. Anita didn't seem to be upset. She merely said that they would be back in few minutes. We sat on the bench and continued our conversation. Before long Fuchs and Helen reappeared. It was getting late and we had to return to the barracks. We shook hands and departed. On the way to the barracks, I told Fuchs excitedly about Anita; that she was very pretty and very pleasant. He interrupted me with a question: "Did it go pretty good?" Yes, I thought, it went well.

Several days later, Fuchs approached me and told me that he had received a written card from Helen through a messenger, asking us to meet them tonight around ten o'clock. It was extremely dark that night and cold, with autumn getting closer and closer. We walked around for a while and then stopped by a tree. We walked around for some time, and again Fuchs and Helen excused themselves. Anita and I had walked around for a while and stopped by a tree. Before I knew what was happening, she was so close to that I could feel her warm body next mine, her blonde hair in my face. Slowly she raised her head and kissed me hard on my mouth, her whole body pressing ever harder against me. "Georg, ich liebe dich," she whispered. I was scared and yet very excited. Her mouth was very persistent. Slowly, almost unknowingly, my hand found her breasts. She kept whispering. "Georg, Georg, Ich mochte Dich so." Slowly and inevitably we succumbed to our passions and lay down in the grass. Time lost all meaning. I forgot where I was and who I was. Nothing really mattered. This young girl next to me wanted me. That alone was important. Quietly now, whispering to me, she helped me to achieve my manhood. I remember only that I made to the barracks that night; how; I do not know.

Our training continued. Periodically, Captain Kluge would make inspection tour to determine the progress being made, and each time he was satisfied. Then, finally, our last week. Now, we were to learn all about field telephones. Then we would leave and start building our line. Apparently, the word must have gotten around the town, for that afternoon, I received message from Anita; she wanted to see me.

This time I left Fuchs behind and went be myself. We met at our usual spot. For a long time, we walked in silence. Then she said slowly and very quietly. Georg, I don't know where to begin this. Everything happens so fast nowadays. I understand that you are leaving very shortly. Of course, you can't tell me where you're going and possibly, you don't even know yourself. However, please keep in touch with me. I love you very much. Please don't laugh. I know that I'm very young, only fifteen. Yet remember, there is war going on. I know this. Most of our young friends have gone over a year now and some of them will never be returning. This why I believe in grabbing my share of happiness while I have a chance. Please don't think too harshly of me. The past several weeks have been very wonderful. You are so different in many ways; perhaps that too is the war. You are gentle, and I'm glad that I was the first girl in your life. Here, her voice trailed off and she started sobbing quietly. "Please don't cry Anita." My hand was stroking her hair, "We will keep in touch. Perhaps we shall meet someday in the future. Who knows? This is a funny world in which we live." It was getting late now and she stopped her crying. "Georg, let's return to the place where we first made love. Please, I want you so much."

CHAPTER TWENTY-EIGHT

Joining the Battalion
Late Fall 1943

The following week we left for Rumania to start our line. It was a wonderful trip for us. We had our trucks loaded on the train to conserve gasoline, and it took us about four days to get to our destination. Again, we unloaded and moved into a school house. From then on, it was hard work. First, we would go out into the woods and cut down trees for poles. Then the poles had to be carried by hand to the trucks. Then the trucks would follow the road and drop off the poles alongside of the road, regardless how far we were from assigned hole. The poles ranged in height from twenty to forty feet. They weren't too light. From them on, it was a team work. Some people were assigned to digging the holes; others were drilling the holes in the poles for insulators, while still others were getting the wire ready. It was hard work and we were pretty good. One thing I had to say for Sergeant Stutz; he was fair on the job. Each morning he would come out and tell us what objective was for the day. When it was accomplished, we were done, whether it took us six hours, or four hours or even ten hours. We worked our heads off, and generally managed to get in around three in the afternoon, enjoying the rest of the day just loafing and doing our chores.

As soon as we completed our section of the line, we would load up our trucks leap frog other companies on the line and pick a new section to be completed. This went on for several weeks until finally arrived in Hungary. This was really a beautiful country, very flat and very friendly. Here again, we worked hard and always managed to get off in time to go to the local village to have some fun. Unfortunately, however, this could not last too long. Soon, the taste of war returned to us in full force. One day we were riding in our trucks, enjoining the weather, glad that we could quit early since so much needed to be done at the base. I sat on the bench, my mind thousand miles away, when suddenly I heard someone scream; enemy aircraft. Without even thinking, I jumped off the truck and rolled into a ditch; Not a minute too soon. I saw four American P-40 fighters flying approximately at five hundred feet above the ground, their machine guns blazing. One of the truck careened crazily, hit an embankment, and rolled on its side. In a flash, it was enveloped in flames. Fortunately, everyone managed to escape it. The planes had made several passes while we glued ourselves to the sides of the ditch. Then they were gone as suddenly as they arrived. Cautiously we climbed out of the ditch to see what damage had been done. Two trucks were destroyed. One had several holes in the cab, but nothing appeared to be seriously damaged. Several men had slight wounds from the bullets. Anxiously we moved from one truck to another, looking, hoping we would not find any bodies. Then I saw him, just a step away from the ditch. He lay face down, as though afraid to look up, his back covered with blood. His arms were outstretched as though as though he was saying, "please, not me, I am your friend." Fuchs had finally met his maker. I knelt next to him, trying to comfort him, though I knew that he was dead.

The following morning, we were given permission to take time off to bury Fuchs. A local cemetery was selected for the burial and we carried the casket into the graveyard. The rest to the company followed behind us. Each individual was engrossed with his own thoughts, wondering perhaps how much more time he had left, on this earth and how to best to utilize it. Lieutenant Kluge delivered the eulogy, short and yet very forceful. He decried the necessity for this needless killing, and of a boy who had to give up his life far away from home because believed in this cause. Fuchs would have laughed at this. What cause? A Neuses Europe? I stayed a little longer at the grave. He was such a good friend. Why did he have to leave me? "So, long Pal," I whispered through clenched teeth. Then I walked away, leaving him behind.

From that day on, we made sure that some body was awake and watching all time for American aircraft. I remember getting caught while making a tie on the pole. I spotted P-40 flying very high. The next time I saw it; it was approximately 500 feet off the ground, its machine guns blazing. There was only one thing to do in situation like this, grab hold of the pole kick your climbers free, and slide down the as fast you can. This time we were very fortunate, no one was hurt; only Sergeant Kline was upset; he was caught in the open field and had run like mad for the ditch with the aircraft in hot pursuit, while the rest of us sat under the poles, laughing our heads off. Several days later one of our trucks was destroyed. Luckily, this it was empty. The driver had managed to jump into the ditch and escaped with few minor bruises.

Under these conditions, the work was ever more difficult and yet we tried hard to preserve our sense of balance. We worked hard, everyone pitching in, hoping to get the job done and return home early to go about the town. However, things were not going smoothly, Sergeant Stutz kept harassing us continuously at every opportunity calling us "untermenschen" (sub humans), someone much lower than the German race. His curses, "Blades Volk", damn stupid foreigners, were extremely difficult to take at times.

We spent many hours at night pleading with some of the hot heads to avoid any kind of trouble at all costs. Things were going well, and at least we ate hot meals. We worked hard, true, but we had a certain amount of freedom. Nobody bothered us at night. There wasn't any sense in upsetting the equilibrium because of an idiot like Stutz.

These sessions proved to be important for all of us. Since Fuchs was gone, the faith of our compatriots had in us had deteriorated somewhat. Fuchs was typical big city boy, cocky and reckless; he could not help but command a certain respect and envy. The rest us, while from the same city, were much quieter. As for me, I almost didn't count, since I was not only the youngest, but also the shortest. I finally got lucky one night; a young man came up to me and said, I'm from Lwow; I am probably couple years older than you, but I would like to be your friend; my name is Stan; we shook hands; things got easier for me; Stan would warn me of any problems that were on horizon. As time went on, I noticed that Sergeant Rice and the older driver, an Austrian by the name of Wilhelm Goerner, continued to stay aloof and did not take part in harassment of us. I remember one occasion when Sargent Klein grabbed one our man for some silly reason and ordered him to run and hit the prone position. At first, we thought it was very funny to watch Klein foaming at the mouth, ordering him; "hin legen, auf march march." But when the boy became so exhausted that he could no longer get up and he refused the order. Klein broke into profanity about the "Blades Volk." This was too much.

We all started forward, encircling Klein and his victim. At first, he didn't notice anything. But then he realized that something was amiss; he saw us all around him, just staring at him and daring him to do something. His face turned ashen. In high pitched voice, he screamed at us "hereaus, geh weg." Nobody moved. We just stared at him. His hand moved nervously toward his service pistol. From the corner of my eyes I looked at Rice and Goerner. They both stood by the truck, totally indifferent, Rice a little amused at the performance, enjoying Klein's predicament and wondering what would happen next. I too wondered. This was the first time that I realized the seriousness of our situation. Should something happen to Klein, we would really be in a jam, but it was too late now to turn back.

Yarbor disengaged himself from the group. Slowly, he walked to the boy on the ground; he lifted him to his feet and helped him past the group to the truck. There was complete silence. No one uttered a sound, each one waiting for the next move. Klein must have realized that he had lost. He turned quickly and stormed past us and past the truck, going in the direction of the town. We watched him for a long time angrily stomping the ground, walking in the direction of the Headquarters. I figured he was on his way to report to Stutz about the incident. Slowly the group broke up, and walked toward the truck. Rice was smiling now. "Sehr gut," he said. "Klein ist ein schwein." With this he told us get the group ready; we had work to do.

That night the four of us were called into Stutz office. We walked in, saluted and remained standing. Stutz was sitting at the head of the table, his face twisted in an angry grimace. Rice and Klein were sitting on either side of him, while the other members were sitting in the rear. We stood in silence for a long time, Stutz just looking at us, moving his eyes constantly. Suddenly, he exploded. "It was all your fault. You could have prevented this incident. You are here to assist us and not to create any mutinies. You have seriously disrupted our discipline and if I have anything to do with it, you will pay dearly for this." His tongue lashing continued for several minutes, condemning us for our heritage and decrying the necessity for a soldier of Third Reich to be associated with such trash.

"Herr Oberfeldwebel ......" Yarbor's voice was quiet, yet visibly restrained. His face was covered with sweat and his lips were quivering nervously. "Herr Oberfeldwebel," he reapeted once more. "It is our desire to speak to the Lieutenant. We have grievances to discuss with him." Stutz was stunned at first, but then he really exploded. He jumped from behind the back of the table and stormed toward us. For a while I thought that he was going to walk right over us. He stopped in front of Yarbor, his right hand clinched, and for a few seconds they just stared at each other. Then Stutz quietly started talking to us, calmer now but very forceful. "I'm in command here. You will do as I say or you will be destroyed. You are nothing. You are dirt under my feet. You aren't fit to live." "Herr Oberfelfeber, you may say all you want; you may threaten us all you want. We came here with a request to see and speak with the Lieutenant. Please give us your answer, yes or no." Stutz turned to me with a look of disbelief. He cursed angrily and shouted. "What is going on? I have given you my answer. You report to me and no one else." Herr Stutz, we will not talk to you; we still want to talk with the Lieutenant. If you will not grant us permission, we will go to see the Captain." This was too much. "Heraus," he screamed at the top of his voice. We had no choice; the interview was over. We walked outside. Yarbor could no longer control himself. "That son of a bitch. Tonight, he will get it. It' a good thing that I kept the pistol. He won't get away with this."

Quickly we grabbed him and dragged him away from the building. "Listen, we are on your side, but it would be suicide to do this. "He has witnesses; they would know immediately who did this. That bastard will pay for this. Let's wait couple of weeks. During the next air raid, when everyone is looking for cover, that is the time we get the son of a bitch." Slowly he quieted down. He sat on the ground with his head in his hands. "My God, I hate that man with everything that I have. What have we ever done to him? Just because he was Polish once, why does he take it out on us? "We silenced quickly as we heard footsteps approaching us in the darkness. Soon the figure of Unteroffizier Rice appeared among us.

He motioned for me to join him, and started to walk away. Quickly, I followed him down the path. "Boy, you are in trouble," he began without any preliminaries. "I'm not going to tell you what to do. I just want you to know that I sympathize with you boys. I have been very happy here with you. I have nothing but praise for you. You work hard and lead as a normal life as you can under the circumstances. What I'm trying to say is just be careful in the future. Unfortunately, Stutz is in command here and that swine Klein is his pet. Before you decide to do something drastic just remember that you are subject to military jurisdiction. You wouldn't stand a chance. You are needed here; when I say you, I mean all four of you. Could you imagine what would happen to the rest of the boys if you weren't here? You owe this to them. You must make your grievances known. Don't give in to Stutz now. The next time the captain is here, after his speech, just request permission to talk to him from the ranks. That way Stutz will not be able to silence you." With this he patted me on the back and left. Slowly I returned to the group and related to them my conversation with Rice. We decided to take his advice, and I was selected to approach the captain during his next visit.

CHAPTER TWENTY-NINE

Field Deployment
Late Fall 1943

The next few days went on without an incident. Stutz avoided us and of this we were glad. Klein was nowhere to be found, gone to Headquarters, I supposed. Then on Sunday we were called out. Captain had arrived and wanted talk to us. I started with much anxiety; this was to be my day. In the hall, we bumped into Rice. Quickly he whispered to me that he had told the Captain that I would act as his translator today. Thank God, I said to myself as I came out smiling. This was going to be easy.

As I walked out of the building, the company was already assembled. Sergeant Stutz called the company to attention and reported to the Captain. They exchanged salutes, the company was put "at ease," then motioned to me to come forward. I approached the Captain and saluted. I gave him my name and moved over to his left side. Captain was smiling, obviously in a happy frame of mind. His beginning threw me off guard. "Gentlemen, I have been watching your progress diligently. You have done well. Let me be the first to congratulate you for a job well done. I anticipated a lot of trouble from you because of your nationality and because of your age. Yet, you proved me wrong. For this I thank you. You can be proud of being a part of this unit, a position you have earned."

I looked at faces in front of me; they were grinning. It was a pleasure to hear something good for a change. I too began feel good. "You have undergone many hardships, Captain continued, "but you have endured them without complaining. His voice was quieter now, "you have suffered your first casualty not too long ago. Believe me I share your loss. Fuchs was a good man and we all miss him very much. But, we cannot grieve; the war must go on and we must do our part in the struggle. I am very happy to announce that the Fuhrer has fulfilled his promise to the Third Reich. We now have the weapon he promised, and even now, England is being shelled with this terrible weapon. Its name is "V-1." It is a rocket, full of explosives. It takes off from the ground and flies with the help of an engine. Then over the target, the engine shuts off, and the bomb falls to the earth. We will repay England for the shameful and disgraceful destruction of our cities, and for the thousands of civilians who have given their lives during the air raids. The victory will be ours." His voice now at feverish pitch. "Sieg," he cried. Caught by his enthusiasm, We replied, "Heil." The meeting was over and the company was dismissed. My comrades were hanging back, ready to assist me in the event I needed help. "Herr Captain," I spoke softly to the Captain. "May I have few words with you, sir?" "Certainly", he replied. His humor was gay. From the corner of my eyes I noticed that Stutz had turned white; the bastard knew what was about to happen. "Sir, I respectfully request your permission to speak you on behalf of this unit." "Yes, son, continue." He stopped now, looking at me intently.

"Sir, let me tell you that we appreciate your wonderful comments and your confidence in us. We realize that we have a job to do and that it is very important. We also realize that we enjoy relative freedom, for which we thank very sincerely. We take our hardships without complaint because we know that there are soldiers on the front lines in Russia who are subjected to much greater hardships. And yet, they bear them without complaint in view of the greater things at stake. But, sir, there is one thing that I would like to bring to your attention. We are foreigners; we didn't ask to be here. We were brought here against our wills in most cases. We have accepted the situation and decided to make the best of it. As you mentioned, we have worked hard and caused very little concern. However, we don't like to be treated like second-rate people." Here I stopped, wondering if I had gone too far. The Captain looked at me quizzically. "What are trying to say?" He inquired softly. Quickly I went into a detailed explanation of the incident of few days ago.

"Sergeant Stutz, I want everyone connected with this incident brought into your office in the next ten minutes. Is that clear?" His voice was cold now. Stutz nodded and departed. I followed the Captain into the office. When we were, all assembled, the Captain asked me who else from the cadre was present when Sergeant Klein put on his exhibition. Haltingly, I spoke Sergeant Rice's name. "Herr Rice, you have heard the complaint. Is there anything you wish to add or correct?" "Nein, Herr Haupman," was the quiet reply. "Her Stutz," was wollen sie zagen?" Again, the voice was very cold and unfamiliar. Stutz started to say something, then fell silent."Ich kann sie night horen," Captain persisted. "Her Haupman, Ich habe nichts zu zagen." His voice was loud, betraying no emotions. "Was this case brought to the attention of the Lieutenant"? "Nein." The reply was quick but short. "Then am I to assume that what this young man has related to me is the absolute truth?" The tone of his voice was merciless. Again, only silence. The Captain started pacing around the room, his right arm hanging uselessly by his side. Suddenly, he stopped in from of Sargent Klein. "People like you make me ashamed that I am a German. You are a pig, Sergeant.

Now listen to me very carefully. I want you apologize to these boys here and now." Klein's face was ashen. Through clenched teeth he managed to utter, "Verzeihung sie mine Herren." Her Stutz, I want you to prepare an order dismissing Sergeant Klein from this unit. He is to report Battalion Headquarters immediately to volunteer for front line duty. Are there any questions?" I looked at Stutz and I was shocked at the hate in his eyes. Rice was right; This man will never forgive me or any or anyone of us for this. From now on it is war between us, and somehow, I was glad. I too felt only extreme hate for him.

Several days later I had an opportunity to speak with Rice. Quickly I apologized to him for bringing his name the attention of the Captain, thus placing him in disfavor with Stutz. "Don't worry, son," he replied quietly. "I hate these half-Germans with a passion. But you boys had better be careful; he is out to get you." Klein had left immediately after the formation and we apparently had seen the end of him. His replacement arrived a couple of days later, a young Austrian boy by the name of Kurt Hoffman. He was Unterofficier, and a veteran of the front. Half of his instep was shot off. He was a nice man who had always had a kind word to say to everyone and appeared happy to be with us rather than be back at the front lines. Conditions certainly improved for us.

CHAPTER THIRTY

Deployment to Hungary
Fall-Winter 1943

During this period however, the Allied bombings kept increasing in intensity and it was constant battle for survival; dodging 50 mm machine-gun bullets from P-40's fighters or jumping into air raid shelters to avoid bombs directed at our parked vehicles. We were still on the move to our destination in Hungary. This seemed to be such a pleasant country. The people were very nice to us, and it was enjoyable to walk down the street and be able to purchase whatever you wanted without benefit of ration cars. Of course, we didn't have any money, but that was beside the point.

Slowly our line progressed, and we kept leap frogging other companies, trying desperately to finish the job. The worst scare we had so far was the night travel. Since we couldn't risk losing anymore trucks to the air attacks, decision was made to move at night. Of course, this too presented problems. The Hungarian and Czechoslovak underground was very active, and one never knew when they would strike. I thought the situation was very ironic. It wasn't too long ago that I was engaged in similar operations, and now I was having to defend myself against them just because I was riding in a German vehicle and was wearing a German uniform. These were tense moments, but thank God, we were spared direct attacks. We heard many reports however, of members of our other Companies caught on the highways and were destroyed. During all night movements, each truck carried a German Cadre man with machine pistol. We always tried to sleep on the floor to get a little protection. I guess we were fortunate. Nobody ever bothered us.

Finally, we came close to Budapest and that Sunday we were given day off for outstanding performance in construction of the line. We got all cleaned up and were taken in trucks to the city for sightseeing. It was quite a trip. The city was simply beautiful. Late in the afternoon, tired but happy, we were returning to our camp, when suddenly Hoffman cried out, "Enemy aircraft"! While the trucks were still moving, we were jumping off over the sides, just looking for a place to hide. The peaceful afternoon turned into a nightmare. There were four aircraft attacking, and they seemed determined to make sure that nobody would walk away from this. Of three trucks we had with us, two were already burning and the third one was in in a ditch with bodies jumping over the sides. All this time, the aircraft were flying down the road, taking a wide turn to the right, and returning for another pass. They were having a picnic. Bombs were exploding and the machine guns were just chattering away endlessly. My immediate thought was to get into one of the bomb craters; no two bombs ever land in the same place. I had almost made it when suddenly I heard the awful whistle, the sound of it pushing me into the ground. Then came the loud explosion and the force of it just picked me up threw me against something. My mind went blank. So, this was finally the end. I was thankful for one thing; it happened very fast and quite painlessly. My ears were ringing madly. I couldn't hear anything nor did I understand what had happened. I was certain that I was dead. I don't know how long it was before the noise and the roar of the bombs and the screams and machine guns subsided, but suddenly all was quiet again. Occasionally I could hear a moan of pain from bodies lying on the ground. I looked around me. The entire landscape had an eerie look. The trucks were destroyed and still burning. There were bodies on the ground lying perfectly still; others were writhing and moaning.

Slowly it dawned on me that I too was among the living. I tried moving my limbs; my left arm wouldn't move. So, I guess that's it. Not too bad after all. I suppose the concussion had slammed me against a tree and the only damage so far was a broken arm. I could have been much worse. Slowly I got up and started walking around trying to give some assistance. By this time, several others joined me; while we were all bloody, at least we were moving. Slowly we approached the first truck. It was still burning. We counted eight dead, and several others wounded and in need of medical attention. I sent couple of people in opposite direction to stop traffic and bring some ambulances. I was completely unaware of pain as I kept walking from truck to truck, looking and hoping to be able to help the wounded. Then it occurred to me that I have not seen Yarbor. Please God, not him; not another one. I was running now. I had to find him. He wasn't among the bodies and the wounded around the trucks; he must have escaped. Good. I heard someone crying for help in the ditch. Quickly I followed the sound, with several men following me. One of the boys had several wounds and was bleeding very badly. Someone else stopped to take care of him, while I continued to search for Yarbor.

I heard more moans and quickly ran in that direction. There he was, almost in the ditch, his back covered with blood. There were several ugly holes staring me in the face. He was awfully pale and weak. When I bent down over him, he recognized me and smiled weakly. "Well, that's two down. You are the only one left to get home and tell our parents what we have done for the Neues

Europa." His voice was very weak. I told him to be quiet and try to relax, but he merely shook his head. "Don't bother. It won't be long now. Please try to get the message home. Tell them that I am very sorry to leave them, but I really don't have too much of a choice." I lifted him out of the ditch, rested his head in my lap, and placed a moist handkerchief against his lips. "Remember, George, get the word home. You're the last one. You must survive this somehow to tell our people what we have done." OH yes! Don't forget Stutz. That son of bitch doesn't deserve to live. He must be killed. Promise me that you will see that he is taken care of." Even at death's door, his face was livid with hate. His eyes were looking intently into mine. "George, I don't care who does it, but he must be made to pay the penalty for all the suffering and abuse he gave us. You owe this to me and Fuchs. Promise." His hand was gripping mine hard and I could hardly see his face for my tears. My God, why does it always end this way. Why can't I have one friend who manages to survive this misery. "Don't worry Pal, he will be taken care off," I heard myself saying. "My pistol is in my rucksack. Make sure you get there first; otherwise, it will be confiscated." This awakened me. I must not let anyone know that my arm is broken. I must get to our quarters first and get the pistol. After that, it won't matter. But I must not let them put me on the ambulance. I looked at Yarbor. He was very quiet now. His breathing was getting weaker and weaker, and blood was oozing from his mouth. And then I heard him whisper so quietly that I had to strain to hear him. "George, I'm so frightened. What will happen to me? It has been such a long time since I have been to church. I don't want to end up in hell." I couldn't remember words for the act of contrition. I just made up my own prayer. "Please God, accept his soul. He is so young and yet has been exposed to so much that is evil. Be patient with him, for he will be joining you soon. Please don't punish him, oh Lord and permit him to enter your kingdom and achieve the final peace. Forgive him Father all his sins; please Father, give him peace." Once more he looked at me. He was smiling now. "They aren't going to get their damn "Neues Europa" after all. They are finished. They will pay dearly for all the suffering they have imposed on the world. It is a shame that I won't be around to see it, but no matter, I know the outcome, that is enough." He started coughing very badly. "Please, Pal, just relax. You're going to be OK." Oh sure I am. He looked at me, his eyes full of pain and anxiety. "Don't forget Stutz, don't let us down." His last words were almost inaudible. Then he was gone.

Later on, the ambulances arrived at the scene and those needing medical attention were driven to a nearby military hospital. Somehow I managed to hide my injury; it wasn't sore anymore. I boarded a truck with others and returned to the camp. I went immediately to Yarbor's rucksack and went quickly through his clothing and other belongings. There, on the bottom was the pistol. I slipped it into my pocket and went looking for my friends. They were lucky, they had decided to sleep instead of going to Budapest. I told them the whole story and went on. "Well, so now we are three. Who is going to take care of Stutz? I have the pistol. Anytime any of you want it, just let me know. However, I still think that we must prepare for this very carefully. Remember, it has to be done right, or we will jeopardize everyone here. You know damn well right that they aren't going to stand by and see one of their own killed, regardless of how bad this bastard is." To this we all agreed. It was decided that the plan would be formulated later; the time was not yet ripe.

It was getting late, so I decided to go to bed. Sometime during the night I woke up with an awful pain; apparently I must have rolled over on my arm. It hurt like hell. The remainder of the night was hell, and I welcomed the first sign of the daybreak. After we were awakened I reported to the medic and told him about my injury. He examined me and said that I would have to go to the hospital to have a cast placed on my arm.

CHAPTER THIRTY-ONE

Military Hospital
Fall-Winter 1943

I n a way, the next four weeks were wonderful. I was admitted to a General Hospital, where I was the youngest patient and the only foreigner there. Everyone treated me like a little child. They spoiled me rotten. Each afternoon we were allowed visit the town. It was very pleasant, and my fellow patients were simply marvelous. They seemed to have completely forgotten that I was a member of "Bloedes Volk." They treated me like one of their own. I ate more ice cream in those brief four weeks than I had eaten in my whole life. The activities of the day were food for thought for the night, and I found myself wondering how I could hate these people. They represented everything that I despised and yet they were human. They are suffering a great deal now, and possibly didn't even believe anymore what they heard on the radio or read in the newspapers. I had a strange feeling that some of these guys were hopping that they would not return to the frontline again.

The bed next to me was occupied by Unteroffizier Knopf. The hospital was in his hometown and his wife visited him every day. His right leg was badly shot up and he was in a cast from his hip down; we were a wonderful couple, he was in cast from hip down and I was in cast from waist up. He had been wounded in my home town, Lwow. We spent hours talking about things in general. His father was a principal of a high school in town, and as a matter of fact, Knopf was teaching history before he was drafted into the service. He seemed to be very understanding, and my conversations with him were always very interesting.

One day he invited me to accompany him and meet his father. We met in a restaurant. His father looked distinguished and old. His hair was snow white; his body looked tired. And yet, he was constantly smiling. He seemed genuinely happy to meet me. We talked awhile about the war, and then he mentioned that he too remembered my home town; He was there during WWI. After lunch, he invited me to visit his school and talk to the student body about our schooling system. I was rather hesitant, not knowing what to make of it. Wouldn't somebody object? Knopf must have realized the predicament in which I found myself for he just smiled and said "don't worry, son, you are among friends. I think that you will actually enjoy it."

Couple of days later, in the early afternoon, I made my appearance at the high school accompanied by Knopf. His father introduced him first; some of the students remembered him from the earlier days. He seemed so relaxed and yet so out of place in his uniform. I thought he must have been a good teacher. The kids were laughing over his war stories, some of them deliberately twisted to make the misery of it sound hilarious. "And now, I would like for you to meet a friend of mine who comes from a large city in Poland, whose German name is Lemberg. He is now serving in the Luftwaffe helping us in the war effort. He is very young, and yet he has seen a great deal of the suffering and misery connected with the war. He will talk to you briefly about the school conditions in his native country and then the floor will be open for questions. He will talk to you in German, and I can testify that he does speak our language rather well."

Initially, I was very nervous and scared, but the feeling soon wore off. These students were of my age, eager to find out how we lived and how we felt about the war. The meeting lasted for couple of hours. I was amazed at some of the questions; they were frank. Some of the students were expressing doubts that the war would be won by Germany and were wondering what would happen to people like me, who "volunteered" to serve in German Luftwaffe.

Slowly I managed to tell them my story; how I was captured and how anxious I was to learn where about of my family. I looked at Mr. Knopf Sr. from time to time, trying to ascertain if I was perhaps over stepping the bounds of courtesy, but he merely smiled and kept shaking his head; completely enjoying the show. After couple of hours, he finally got up and told the assembly that due to the late hour, they would have to break but since I was in the hospital nearby, he felt certain that I could be induced to return soon. As I thanked him and the student body, I received a standing ovation; I was overcome with joy. On the way back to the hospital, I asked young Knopf if I said anything that was not acceptable. He looked at me and said, "George, you will learn that we Germans aren't as bad as you make us out to be. We have our faults, of course, but basically, we believe in the same things you do. Unfortunately, our system is of a different conviction and we will pay very dearly for this someday. Don't you realize that I couldn't have gone through all those months on the front without being exposed to some of the things that you mentioned? Don't you think that I know what was being done to the Jews in Poland? Yet, what can I say? I swore allegiance to the Fuehrer. What can I say? I am a non-commissioned officer in the German Army. I must obey orders regardless of the consequences. This is our Prussian code; blind obedience to our superiors. They know what is right and what is wrong."

He sounded so bitter he couldn't really believe in what he told me; of this I was certain. And yet, how could he really raise a voice against what was going on? He had a wife and ten-year-old boy to feed at home. Was he justified of feeling noble? Should he forsake his family and fight the cause on his own? No. It would have been completely hopeless. The concentration camps were full of people like him; it was better to have him out, discussing the feelings with others, being very careful of course. People would listen to him. After all, he was a teacher and he was a soldier; he had been on the front lines and had seen with his own eyes the events he talked about.

I returned to the school several times and each time I enjoyed it immensely. In addition, I was invited to Knopf's house for dinner couple of times and really enjoyed the conversations with the older and the younger Knopf's. At home, they were completely relaxed and their questions were frank and to the point. It was with much regret that I awaited my release from the hospital to rejoin my unit. But after all, I had been gone almost five weeks; my arm was completely healed and the cast was off. A couple of more days and I would leave. When the time came, I went into the ward to say goodbye. I had gotten to know these guys rather well. They were all together here, all united. They were all just patients, whether SS, Luftwaffe or Wehrmacht, and as such, fine friends. I hated to leave them. I stopped by to see Knopf. H held my hand for a long time.

"Boy, keep your eyes open and remember what you saw in this hospital and in town. Basically, we are decent people. Think about what you have seen here before you start condemning us as a Nation. We all must share in the guilt, yet, we must share proportionately. Just remember this. If you ever come this way after the war, stop by and visit with us. Pop will be glad to see you." I shook hands warmly with all the patients in the ward and then got ready to leave. My unit was in Bratislava and now I would have to proceed by train on my own. It was utterly amazing. The great German bureaucracy was all fouled up. Here I was, a force laborer, and I was being sent by train all by myself in search of my unit. But then, where could I run to? I really had no choice but to find my unit and see what would come next.

I was quite excited at the prospect of a train trip on my own; it sounded thrilling and important. As I approached the railroad station, I was a bit uncomfortable, somehow feeling that I would soon feel the hand of Gestapo or Feld Gendarmerie on my arm asking who I was and where I was going. But nothing happened; as a matter of fact, I was totally ignored. By the time the train started, it was already dark. It was crowded beyond description, with bodies everywhere you could possibly fit one. Our train was equipped with an anti-partisan unit, which meant that in front and rear were flat cars equipped with several quad-20 mm cannons plus some submachine guns. If the train were attacked by low flying aircraft, the quad 20's would provide more than adequate protection. If, on the other hand, it was attacked by partizans, they too would have some difficulty, for the sides of the flat cars were built up with steel plates, the offering plenty of protection for the crew.

After couple of hours' ride, an Officer came through the cars advising us that we were now in the area where partisans were most active and told us to get our weapons ready. Nobody would leave the train unless ordered by a car Commander appointed in each car. I was little afraid, wondering what would happen if the train were attacked, but after looking around, I found that most soldiers were totally unconcerned and just went back to sleep. I took my usual position for the trip; next to the window. I wasn't about to miss anything. I wanted to see where I had been and where I was going. The trip proved to be very uneventful, not even an air raid.

CHAPTER THIRTY-TWO

Bratislava - Bavaria
Winter 1943

When I arrived in Bratislava, I immediately reported to the local Luftwaffe Headquarters with my papers. They looked at me with amazement, first curious and then laughing. I suppose my German speech really broke the ice for me. I was fed well and really enjoyed my situation, for no one really knew what to do with me. They heard about my unit, but where it was at present time, nobody seemed to know or cared. And so, for the next couple of days I just sat at the Headquarters, eating, sleeping and enjoying my trips into town in the afternoon. I think Bratislava is about the cleanest city in the world; it was simply beautiful, situated on the bank of Danube river. Then finally, one day the Germans decided that I had been there long enough. They made a serious attempt to locate my unit. They were, unfortunately successful and later that day I was placed in a command car and driven to my unit which was located about 25 miles outside the city.

It would be good to see the old gang; of course, at the time of day when I got there, they were still working on the line. I walked into the office and reported in. Stutz greeted me with very little enthusiasm, I suppose he felt that another trouble maker had returned to make things more difficult for him. I just wondered around, enjoying the temporary freedom of trying to get used to the idea of being a member of the working company once more. It was a strange feeling, and yet I was glad to be back. I wondered how many more of my friends had gone to the meet their maker. I hoped that they were still in good shape.

Sometime later, I heard the trucks drive up; the old gang was back. Quickly I ran down the steps to greet them. Before I had a chance to say anything, I was surrounded by my friends, all talking at once, wondering what I had been doing and why in the hell I wanted to return. Laughingly I quieted them down and invited them to sit around my bunk while I told them about my days away from the company. Several others joined in, and I suppose I must have talked for about an hour. It was very pleasant feeling. I knew that I belonged here, and that they were glad to see me back despite what they said.

Then came their turn. Things have not been going well. The work was getting harder, and now Sundays had been declared as a regular work day. Everything for Neues Europa. Several boys were killed by raiding P-40's. I knew them of course, but none too well. The weather was getting cold and sickness took its toll. We only had one set of clothing and two sets of underwear. We had to wash them constantly to avoid lice, we were forced sometimes to wear damp clothing. This of course didn't help in the cold weather. Soon it was time for bed. As the guys hit for their bunks, I noticed Stan hanging back. He embraced me and welcomed me back. After few words, he became serious. George, he said, "You have no idea how we missed you. You are our Hero." After your session with the Captain and the dismissal of the Pig, Klein; we adopted a new nick name for you." Here he stopped and smiled; "you went from Flea to Little Caesar." These guys worship you. Again, he hugged me and said quietly, "let's keep in touch."

The next morning, I joined the company on the line. I was excited all day. It had been quite some time since I had done any physical work and I was eager to get back and get started. It was miserable day. It had been raining all day and all night. I was assigned as a climber and walking down the line over the fields wasn't as exciting as I thought. My shoes were so muddy that it was difficult to lift my feet. My trousers were soaked from the wet poles. Great, what a day to get started. I could almost feel pneumonia setting in. This went on for several days. I noticed that Stutz had kept his distance from us and that the food wasn't too bad. We were left pretty much alone, and if we did our job, nothing was said. Then a couple of days later we have completed our task and started break up the camp. Again, it was time to leave. This time, however, we would go by truck. We were headed for the Alps and I thought it was wonderful. I always did want to see them.

During the ride, I noticed that all my friends managed to get a seat on same truck with me. Sometime during the night, I was awakened. Olijnik stood over me and motioned for me to be quiet. Quickly I looked around. Trud was also awake, sitting on the tail gate. Everyone else in the truck was asleep. Slowly I crawled toward the tail gate. Olijnik apologized for waking me up, but this was an opportune time to take some plans. Stutz apparently suspected something, for he never accompanied us on the work detail any more. So, our chances of getting to him unnoticed were getting slim. Since we were riding in the truck now, and since the possibilities of getting caught by Allied aircraft was good, they decided that something should be done to prepare for any eventuality. One thing was clear; Stutz had to be taken care of, no matter what else happened. Yes, I had almost forgotten about it. Yet, knew full well that we could not rest until he got his due.

I didn't have the slightest doubt that before the end of the war, Stutz would be a dead man. Quietly we discussed several plans. The idea of sabotaging the truck he was riding in was abandoned; too many of our men would be hurt. We had to kill him alone, when there would be no possibility of something going wrong. Again, we decided on using the pistol during an air raid. The combination of these two things just had to work out. Then came the question who would do it. I suppose we all wanted to destroy him, and yet, when the time for us to speak up, we decided to flip for it. Olijnik would get the honor. Fortunately, I lost, and the oldest man was chosen by the fate to be the executioner. Trud handed the pistol to him. He took it into his hands, silently working the slide; checking its operation and making sure that a bullet was in the chamber. He put the safety on and placed the pistol inside of his jacket. Quietly we shook hands and went back to our places on the floor.

The next day, we arrived at our destination high in the mountains. It was bitter cold, but the scenery was beautiful beyond description. The mountains rose majestically skyward. Half way up the slopes were covered with small pine trees, but the peaks themselves were free of vegetation, looking tall, uninviting, and proud. Because the community in which we found ourselves was very small, the company was broken into several small groups, and we all quartered in the barns of local farmers. We slept in the hay and I was surprised how warm one could keep in the hay.

CHAPTER THIRTY-THREE

Bavarian Alps
Winter 1943

We spent next several days chopping down trees for the poles. Later, we went out to dig holes for the poles. This was most difficult job, since most every hole had to be dynamited. This seemed routine, however, some of our more resourceful men managed to steal dynamite charges and blasting caps. Later that night we went fishing in the Inn River. We had heard that dynamite makes wonderful weapons against fish. We knew how to prepare charges, but had no idea what size charges to use. After much discussions, a compromise has been reached. The charges were prepared and quickly thrown, creating a graceful arc in the air before making quiet splashes in the water. For a moment there was silence, which was suddenly shattered by the explosions as geysers of water shot skyward. I felt certain that the blasts had been heard twenty miles away. As the sprays dissipated, we could see the water full of stunned fish, floating stomach up. Quickly we waded in and grabbed all we could; we knew damn well that it wouldn't be too long before someone would show up to find out what all the noise was about. The fish were quickly stashed in a brook close to us. Several of the boys dug holes in the shallow water to use as refrigerators. The fish were wrapped in cloth and deposited in the holes; quickly they were covered up and we returned to our barns.

The blast had awakened everyone and they were all asking what happened. Our German cadre came running with their weapons, ready to repulse any parachute attack. It all had an air of comedy but we didn't dare to laugh. The search continued toward the river and it wasn't too long before they all returned. Stutz was leading the parade, and behind him came Rice, still amused, laughter showing around his mouth. Stutz immediately advised us that there would be formation in five minutes. I hurriedly sought out Olilnik and told him to hide his pistol immediately, sensing that a thorough search was forthcoming.

I was right. Stutz was furious; he screamed and cursed until his breath failed him. He accused us of thievery and everything else he could think of. He saw all the dead fish in the river and had quickly put two and two together. He demanded that excess dynamite be returned to him at once; nobody would go to sleep unless he had it all in his hands. While he talked, the remainder of the cadre were going through our clothing, searching. What fools they were, we had learned the hard way not to trust them. Our supplies were safely buried next to the bridge that crossed the brook. However, we just played game with them. This went on for couple of hours until finally Stutz exhausted all his patience. He quickly called my name and I stepped forward. "Where is the dynamite," he asked angrily. "What dynamite?" I asked innocently. Before I had chance to say anything else, I was lying on the ground. His fist caught me squarely in the face. Then his heavy boots were on me. I don't know what would have happen to me had it not been for Hoffman and Rice. They both dragged Stutz away and formation was dismissed.

Olijnik and True anxiously bent over me. My face must have looked like a mess; it was all bloody and I was numb from pain and fear. True just kept repeating; "that bastard is going get it tonight if it's the last thing I ever do. He must be destroyed." Olijnik forced him to shut up; there were several people around and this was no place to make threats. When the medic arrived, he looked at me unconcerned, opened a bottle of iodine and began cleaning my face. I must have screamed my head off from pain. It was discovered that my nose was broken. After the medic had taken care of me, I was allowed to go to sleep. Olijnik and True were both waiting for me. "Listen, I think that dynamite would do a much neater job," Trud stated. Use it as a hand grenade. This way there wouldn't be any questions."

It was a good idea. For next few days Trud was busy timing fuses. He didn't want to have grenade explode in his face, but on the other hand, he didn't give Stutz any warning. It had to be a perfect toss, if he missed, we were all dead. After several tries, Trud was satisfied. The charge was prepared and the only thing we had do is wait for the right opportunity. It came quicker than we expected. One day we managed to return from the line very early and just as we drove into the yard, the air raid sirens went off. Quickly we dispersed. Now it was a question of finding Stutz and follow him. He was running toward the side of the hill. Excellent! We couldn't miss his tall body. He was trying to get away from the parked vehicles. Smart bastard, but this wouldn't help. Once over the ridge he stopped, and pressed his body against the slope. The sky was full of B-24's apparently destined for some big raid somewhere in Germany. However, the Germans had placed some flak units high on the mountains and apparently caught the formation by surprise, for it broke up. Now the time came for the fighters, as one after another came streaming toward the anti-aircraft batteries, the noise from dropping gasoline tanks sounding like a thousand bombs. From their wings came stream of bullets from machine guns. We watched in amazement; it was the first time we had ever seen anything like this. We had completely forgotten about Stutz.

But the aircraft decided to investigate what had caused all this commotion, and naturally, when the trucks were spotted, all hell broke loose. The cannon rounds were falling all around us and were blasting trucks. They were all on fire. The noise of exploding cannon rounds, and the roar of engines as the planes pulled away were deafening. All through this we could hear screams of the wounded. I looked around for Trud but he was gone; quickly I looked to the right just in time to see him disappear over the ridge. Then everything became quiet except for the moan of the wounded. Soon the aircraft returned for the second pass. Again, the machine-guns and the cannons. The ground shook. I didn't dare to raise my head, as I pressed my body tightly against the ground, hoping to mold myself into the hill. Then, just as suddenly as it begun, the raid was over. Slowly we came to our feet. Our barn was gone; the trucks were all burning. Several dead men were lying around the trucks and the barn. Our quiet Austrian driver would never see his children again; he died right next to his truck. Rice had a bloody face and his right arm seemed to be pierced by a shrapnel. I looked for Olijnik and Trud and they were both all right. Trud looked tired and very pale. I didn't dare ask any questions.

Slowly a detail was organized to search for dead and help the wounded. I walked with the party looking for the wounded. We started around the barn and kept increasing the area of search to take the entire plateau. My heart beating fast, I approached the place where Stutz had disappeared. He was still there, his body blown and bloody. "Serves the son of a bitch right," I heard a man say bitterly. After the body had been picked up, I rushed to find Rice; he was in charge now. I had to give him a full report. I found him with the medic. He looked much better now; his face had been washed and it really didn't look too bad with few bruises and couple of cuts. His right arm had been patched where the shrapnel had hit him. I reported that I had found Feldfebel Stutz next to a bomb crater; apparently, he was killed trying to find shelter. Rice walked over with me to where the body had been placed. I knew that he was checking for the shrapnel and there wasn't any. Rice just kept shaking his head gently. The minutes dragged like an eternity. "That's too bad;" I heard him say. "But I suppose we all must go some day." This ended the investigation. As far as anyone was concerned, Stutz had been killed by a bomb.

CHAPTER THIRTY-FOUR

Bavarian Alps
Spring - Summer 1944

The next few days were full of surprises. Rice was promoted to Stutz's position. His first order was to split our group into two work details. This was mandated by need of transportation. Replacement trucks were ordered and delivery was scheduled in two or three weeks. One group was assigned to continue working the line while the second group was assigned to work in the woods to cut down trees for the poles. I was assigned to the second group.

During the breaks, Stan and I would get together and plan our escape. The Germany was finished. Russian' spring offense was very effective and the German Army was in full retreat. The Allied invasion on June 6th was successful and the second front became a reality. Germany was in chaos - highways going west were jammed with refugees and Military transports. Nobody wanted to surrender to the Russians.

All the villages were ordered to build tanks traps to slow down the Allies advance. Those traps were defended by Volk Sturm,

Civilian army of citizens aged 60 plus; they would receive weapons from the local Military.

Our discussions were centered around how many people we could trust to join us in the escape. Our final decision was just me and Stan. We felt that we would have a better chance in the escape by keeping the group small, thus not attracting attention to ourselves. We would bide our time and let the Allies advance into Germany before we would make our escape.

Once our replacement trucks arrived we returned to our standard routine working on the line. We watched large formations of American aircraft flying overhead in direction of Munich and other major cities. Fortunately, we were ignored; they were dropping leaflets depicting current front lines in the West. By mid-summer, Russians were back in Poland - German 6th Army Group in Stalingrad surrendered to the Russians. In the West Allies broke through the Rhineland defenses and were moving East towards Berlin.

Days were flying by, Fall was approaching rapidly and Stan and I started to hoard food - we felt that according to the most recent leaflets, The Allies were advancing toward Salzburg in the south. We were getting ready.

Finally, we made decision to leave while the Indian summer was in the full bloom with a nice warm weather. We made our decision - we would walk away next Sunday night carrying only our food and canteens full of water. We were at minus four days. Were we scared, you bet, but the alternative was worse.

Next Saturday Stan and I had discussion regarding tomorrows upcoming decision. We decided that we would leave individually and meet up couple of miles away from the camp. 11pm was the target time. Whoever gets there first waits until 11pm - if no one shows up at the assigned time, partner assumes the worst and leaves on his own. We shook hands and walked away.

Sunday was a normal working day to help Hitler's "Neues Europa. We came back to the camp after 5pm, cleaned up, and went to dinner. I spotted Stan at the chow line - nodded, and continued. By 9pm it was dark and I sneaked around the German Guard and disappeared in the nearby woods. I carefully walked toward our rendezvous - about 45 minutes later Stan showed up. Without wasting time, we moved out and waked all night to distance ourselves from the camp. We celebrated our first day of freedom by sipping water from our canteens. We were moving SW - so far, it was good.

The first couple of nights passed very uneventfully. At day break we managed to find farmhouses and crawled unnoticed into the barn to get some sleep. It was fortunate that we had managed to save some food - otherwise, I don't know how we would have managed. However, after about three days the food was gone and we decided that it was no longer necessary to walk at night. Food was very difficult to obtain this way, and we decided it would be much better to walk in daytime.

The next day we decided to try and walk in day time. By 4pm that day we were tired, hungry, and very thirsty. We spotted a farm down the road and decided to get some water. As we approached the fence, couple of young girls came to the fence and asked who we were and what we needed; Stan immediately spotted Russian accent and asked the girls if we could get some water and perhaps spend couple of nights in the barn.

The girls led us to the barn and told us to get comfortable. They were working for a lady whose husband was on the Russian Front. They told us that they normally milk the couple of cows at night - they will bring us some food. Sure enough, they appeared around 5pm - brought us some food and a bottle of cider. While we were eating, they were doing their chores - once completed, they joined us and said, "let's get acquainted". They took their dresses off and were stark naked. The younger girl went after me, the other after Stan.

The party lasted a couple of hours. The girls were hungry for sex. There was a shortage of young men in Germany - they were fighting for "Neues Eroupa," Finally, it was time for them to go. Olga, the older one told us to stay in the barn, they would bring us food at noon; "Just keep your manhood ready," she said. After they left I looked at Stan, he had a grin from ear to ear.

This went on for couple of more days, when Olga told us that we must leave. It was a tearful party that night. They brought a rucksack, couple of sweaters and more food. When time was up they both hugged us, and wished us a safe journey. Everyone was crying - we thanked them profusely for their hospitality and the next morning, we were gone.

We decided to follow the highway toward Salzburg the highway was clogged with refugees and military traffic, all moving West, nobody wanting to surrender to the Russians. We took our chances, every so often hitching a ride on some vehicles. The civilian population was very friendly - as soon as they found out that we spoke German, they were more than happy to feed us and talk with us. There was no sense in lying, we merely told them that we were the advance group of our company trying to find the best way to build the telephone line.

Women were particularly affectionate. Always close to tears, they would curse the war for making such young boys leave home to fight. In the same breath, if to answer our thanks, they would reply that they had a son or some other member of the family in the east, and they hoped that our parents were doing the same thing for them. "How the hell we are going to hate this people?" I asked Stan. He merely shook his shoulders. "I guess, even the Germans can be human at times."

Our ride came to an end the next afternoon; we reached a junction about one mile from their destination. We thanked them for the ride and hospitality. The ladies gave us hugs and some food for the road. We walked a few days more until our food gave out. The following day around noon we spotted a German soldier guarding his outpost. He was sitting in a chair his rifle beside him. We decided to pay him a visit and hopefully get some food from him. As we approached him we noticed that he was dead, shut between the eyes by a sniper. We looked around but there was nobody home, probably on patrol looking for Allies soldiers. We took his rations and some money - I looked around and noticed a sign - Vorsicht Minen - Caution mines. I told Stan that we just walked over the mine field protecting the outpost. He just looked at me and shook his head.

We decided that we would walk behind him and then get to the highway. We made sure that we vacated the area on the double. It would not be good to be picked up by his friends with German rations and money. We walked few more days and noticed a road sign, Salzburg 72 miles. We felt good - our goal was getting closer. We were good for about 3 or 4 days with food, so we just kept going hoping for another miracle.

CHAPTER THIRTY-FIVE

On the Run

Fall - Winter 1944

I don't know how long we walked that night, but we wanted to be away as many miles as it was humanly possible between us and the outpost. We didn't do much talking - just walking in silence, looking around and hoping to avoid trouble.

We walked for several days, sleeping and walking, always avoiding major highways. We didn't take any more chances. We hadn't eaten in couple days, and finally, we just couldn't go on. We had to get some sleep, we were totally exhausted. We found a small clump of trees and wormed our way into the bushes.

Our sleep was interrupted by strange noises. We looked up in alarm and found ourselves staring into the face of a strange looking soldier. He was looking at us very curiously, and when he saw that we were awake he said in broken German, "Deutsch, hande hoch."

"Nein, nein, nicht Deutsch, Poland, Poland," we cried anxiously. The soldier looked at us and said in Polish, "A wy tutaj co robicie?" What are doing here?" His question caught us by surprise and we started laughing and crying. This was an American Soldier. We had finally made it. We must have looked like two lunatics, for the soldier was staring at us and saying something to his comrades who approached and encircled us. Finally, half crying, half laughing, we told the soldier who we were and what we were trying to do.

His name was Rudy Kowalski, a second-generation Pole from Pittsburg. He told us that they were on patrol, searching the area for Germans. He said he would have to take us to Headquarters for questioning. Sure - that was fine. This was what we wanted anyway. We must have looked hungry, for he reached into his rucksack and came up with a can of spam and crackers. We were in heaven and emptied the can in no time.

With happy spirits, we followed the group to their lines. When we arrived at the Headquarters, we told the Lieutenant all we knew - also we told him that we would like to remain with the group. Rudy was the interpreter and kept laughing at us. After the questioning, he took us to his platoon area and introduced us to his buddies. They all looked us over and told us to get the hell out of the clothes we were wearing or we might get our tails shut off. They willingly contributed clothing which we changed into after washing them in the nearby creek. It was such a wonderful feeling.

Later, that night we had our feast, cheeseburgers with French fries. The food just kept coming until we told Rudy that we had enough. He just laughed, you boys did good. Rudy told us that we could stay, but we had to hide whenever anyone from another platoon or Headquarters came around, for it was forbidden for them to associate with the civilians.

The next several days were wonderful...... We didn't do much except washing mess kits for the entire platoon. Of course, they fed us, and were nice and pleasant to us. At night, we just sat around the fire, listening to their talk and not understanding a word except, "Okay."

CHAPTER THIRTY-SIX

Life with G.I's

Spring - Summer 1945

The war was still going on, and we moved along with the company, always trying to stay close to Rudy. Without him we were completely lost. No one could understand us and vice versa. Fortunately for us, the battalion was mostly held in reserve for the balance of the campaign. A couple of times we were rushed out at night to help some units in trouble. That, of course, didn't present any problems, since we wore American uniforms. Furthermore, no one really paid any attention to us since it was always at night. We managed to sneak up on the truck and follow the company.

Finally came May 6th, 1945 - The Armistice. We could hardly believe our ears. I threw my hat in the air shouted, "We made it, we made it!" I held Stan in a bear hug and cried my eyes out. Some soldiers gathered around and gave us horrendous applause. We couldn't believe it; the Third Reich was no more - Hitler was dead and the war was over. Two days later, Allied Armies marched into the remainder of Germany. Our unit ended up in Berchtesgaden, Hitler's former retreat.

Now that the war was over, we became accepted by the platoon. Lieutenant Doyle spotted us and wanted to know what in the hell we were doing there. Sergeant Kowalski took him aside and must have really sold him bill of goods, for the Lieutenant came back and smiled at us and told Rudy to tell us something. Rudy translated for us - from now on, the Lieutenant's name will be on the laundry list as well. Yes, indeed! Gratefully we smiled at him.

Several more days went by and Company Commander found out that we were with the company. At first, he raised the roof, but Lieutenant Doyle and Sergeant Kowalski must have convinced him that we were not causing anyone any harm and that, as a matter of fact, we were helping them. He told us that we could stay, but couldn't move with the company, should we get orders to move.

The following Saturday, the company celebrated the Victory over Germany. For the first time, they received an allotment of hard liquor and more beer. Party started at 7pm; we had a local German band and the kitchen provided the snacks. It was a grand Party; There wasn't a dry eye in the place. They all felt good that they have survived the war in one piece and would going home in the near future.

Stan and I were designated as waiters and had a very busy night. Sometime during the night, a soldier claimed the stage and called for quiet. The place went silent; He looked around, took the microphone and started - "Our Father who are in heaven - you could hear the pin drop - when came to the end, his emotions got to him, he whispered 'Amen', and then he said - we have two boys with us who survived the war thanks us - let's give them a big hand." We were asked to stand and the applause went on for quite some time. We just stood there crying and thanking the Lord for our miraculous luck.

The party went on for long time. Rudy made sure that we got to our room OK - we did have a couple beers with the guys and it was prudent to leave when we did. Rudy gave us a big hug and said, "You guys did good and I'm proud of you. Now get some sleep." Stan and I kneeled by our beds and said quiet prayer of thanks for our survival.

Now that we had Company Commander's blessing, we were given a new assignment. We were to work in the kitchen as permanent KP's. These were hilarious days. We couldn't understand a word of English, and some of the cooks weren't too patient, always ending the sentences in a four-letter word and walking away disgustedly to do the chore themselves instead of wasting time trying to explain to us what they wanted. Every time was I given something to do I would seek out Rudy and asking what I was supposed to do. In most cases it worked well, but sometimes I couldn't find him - then the trouble usually started. Slowly, with the aid of sign language and what little we managed to pick up, the situation improved.

CHAPTER THIRTY-SEVEN

Assignment to Tann am Rhon
Summer - Fall 1945

Then came the bad news - the unit was being transferred to small Village approximately 45 miles east of Fulda, Germany on the Russo - American border, to take over patrolling the border. The Captain most emphatically refused to listen to any requests to permit us to go along. We were heart broken. That night he helped Rudy pack his bags, walking around in silence, hoping that tomorrow would never come.

It was early in the morning when the trucks started pull in line for the departure. Platoon after platoon boarded the trucks. We followed the third platoon to their trucks and the last goodbyes were said with tears. We were completely lost, with no idea what we were going to do. Most of the guys came up, shook hands, and said, so long Polski," Rudi was the last one to board the truck. "I tried, boys, but the Old man just wouldn't listen.' We knew this, of course. There wasn't any thing anyone could do.

Then truck engines started and the first trucks began pulling away. Suddenly Lieutenant Doyle jumped off the truck and quickly ran in our direction - without a word he picked me up and threw me into the truck. Stan followed behind me. The truck was moving slowly. The GI's immediately covered us with blankets and gathered around us, hoping to prevent our discovery until it was too late. I squeezed Stan's hand tightly. He looked at me smilingly and said, "We must have been born with a silver spoon in our mouths." "You are so right," I answered weakly.

Several days later after our arrival at the border, we were once again discovered by the Company Commander. He immediately called Sergeant Kowalski and really chewed him out. In the end, however, he gave up and permitted us once again to stay in the kitchen. From then on everything went on smoothly. We started to learn English by reading comic books. Several amusing episodes occurred which I shall never forget.

One of my tasks was to clean the floor in the hallway to the Orderly Room. One of the guys gave me a four-letter word which I should say to the Company Commander as a greeting when he came by each morning. Not knowing any better, I followed his suggestion. Needless to say, the Commander started to chew me out on the spot. I merely grinned at him, not knowing what he was saying. He called for Sergeant Kowalski and told him to tell me what I said. I must have looked like a ghost, for he started laughing. "Just a bad joke, that is all." But from then on I was very careful of what and to whom I would repeat new words which I was not familiar with.

On another occasion, I came into room while one of the guys was opening a package from home. He had a jar of peanut butter. I asked him if it was any good. "Sure," he replied. Then he sent me after some bread. When I returned, he broke a slice in two and piled about an inch of peanut butter on it. Needless to say, once I took a bite I could not open my mouth for the peanut butter. Everyone around just laughed their heads off. To this day, I will not touch peanut butter.

CHAPTER THIRTY-EIGHT

Tann am Rhön

Fall - Spring 1945

Rudy and I became good friends. We spent hours talking about America and Poland. I told him that I had no desire to ever return home. I had no knowledge what happen to my family, and besides, I had no desire to live under Russians again. Soon I was getting letter from his Sister in Pittsburgh, telling me that Rudy had written her all about me and desire to come to the United States. She said that she would initiate action to get me over and that I could stay with them as long as I wanted. This was truly wonderful news, and it made me love Americans even more.

Meanwhile, big changes came to our company. Company Commander and about 30 to 40 guys were rotated to US to be discharged, since their enlistments were about to expire. Their replacements were young men who never did see combat. Their main desires were to get drunk on Saturday night and go out on the streets to beat up on Krauts.

Stan and I decided to act as guardians for the locals. We would stay ahead of the drunk soldiers and warned civilians to seek shelters immediately. We saved several people from getting beat up, unfortunately, some came from back streets behind and walked into mayhem. Word got around, and we were invited to the Mayor's office. We thanked us for our actions and promised us to keep them in house.

One day a German farmed stopped by our Orderly Room; unfortunately, he didn't speak any English, so Captain Doyle, our new Commander called the kitchen and told them send me to see Company Commander. When I got there, Rudi was already there. He pointed at the German and asked me to find out what he wanted.

The German smiled and told me that he has a ranch about ten miles outside the village where he raises vegetables. Unfortunately, wild boar family came from somewhere and were destroying his crops. He asked for some soldiers to kill the boars to save his produce. I related the information to Rudy in Polish, he in turn told Captain Doyle what was needed.

He told Rudi to tell the German that we would like to visit his farm to get an idea of the situation. I got into truck with the Farmer and Captain and Rudi followed us in the jeep. Once we got to the farm, we kind of walked around to get the lay of the land. Since it was getting late, the Farmer asked us to join him and his family for supper. After supper, we set on the porch and watched the sun set.

It wasn't long before we heard the animals. There were five of them. I asked the farmer if they came every night from the same location, he nodded his head. I relayed the information to Rudi who in turn translated it for Captain Doyle. He asked that I tell the farmer that we will be back tomorrow afternoon with the shooters. With this, we said our goodbyes and returned to the company.

The next day, Captain Doyle asked for ten volunteers to shoot the boars. We left shortly after 3pm in a convoy of four jeeps. Once we arrived at the farm, we were introduced to the family and then positioned ourselves directly into the path of the animals and the shooters parked the jeeps. Rudi, I and the family remained the porch. Sun dipped to the west, and before long, it got darker. Captain Doyle again cautioned the shooters to get ready.

It wasn't too long after that we heard the animals. Captain Doyle raised his arm; get ready. Once all five animals cleared the woods, the jeeps turned on the lights; animals were confused - started milling around. The shooters concentrated on the animals, two shooters per animal. The air was filled with exploding rounds. After five minutes, it was over. All animals were dead. The family shook our hands. We took one boar with us to have a wild meat dinner on Saturday night. Everybody was happy. Couple of shooters were from Montana and they volunteered to skin the boar and help the cooks with preparing the feast.

The border patrol duty was boring. Occasionally a group of refugees would be caught and I would be assigned to guard them while they perform various tasks before being shipped to the rear. At first, they mistook me for a German because I spoke their language and they always asked me to help them. But as soon as they found out that I was Polish, they became very close mouthed, knowing full well that no mercy would be shown to them.

During this time, Company was doing a thriving business of bartering with the Russians. They hadn't been paid all through the war, but now they were getting full pay and allowances. However, only portion of it could be taken home; so, they were ready to spend their money. The most popular item was a watch with black luminous dial that sold for between $100 to $125. A bar of candy brought $10. The Russian occupation money was identical to that used in the American Zone, so the Black Market was flourishing.

The Germans were paying $75 for a carton of cigarettes. I often acted as an interpreter on those deals.

This soon came to an end. The German Police and American CID - Criminal Investigation Division, went after black marketers and trade evaporated. By this time, I started learning English using comic books. Some of the words I recognized readily; others were translated for me by the Mess Sergeant, a Czech named Sam. He was very helpful and really encouraged me to learn.

CHAPTER THIRTY-NINE

Journey's End
Summer 1945

As the months went by, Stan and I continued our "Guardian Patrols". I became more involved as a Liaison between Mayor's office and the company. My German was now fluent and my English improved beyond GI talk. Sam has been very helpful in improving my basic vocabulary, which really helped me in my new assignment. Life was very pleasant and peaceful.

Then came the shock. The Division would be going home soon. They were being rotated back to the U.S. Rudi went to see Regimental Chaplain who had befriended on his monthly visits to the Company. Rudy explained my situation to him about his sister's work to sponsor me for a visa to the U.S. It was critical that I be around in case my papers come through. He contacted his friend, Lieutenant Swann, PX Officer, in Fulda, to assign me to work with the crew in the movie theater. Few weeks later, the Division departed for France, and I moved to Fulda. I had many German friends in the Village and made rounds to say good bye.

It was really a great job. I learned all about preparing the reels of film by splicing coming attractions: load the film into the projectors, and finally how to switch reels between projectors. The two guys I worked with were GI's and they treated me like a kid brother. Couple of weeks later, I received telegram from American Embassy in Frankfurt requesting that I visit the Embassy for an interview. Lieutenant Swann made arrangement for me to go to Frankfurt in an ambulance that made daily trip to the hospital there. He accompanied me to the Embassy where we met a very unsympathetic person who wanted to know who I was and who was making the arrangements for my entry into the United States. Lieutenant Swann took all he could and then he blew up. He told the Official that the Company was sponsoring me and that I was to be on the first ship leaving from Bremerhaven. The Official looked a little startled. "We will do all we can," he said.

Several weeks later I received another telegram. This time I was to report to the Embassy to fill out some papers. I got a ride on the truck that was going to Frankfurt to pick up new film that would be shown that night. On the way back, it started to drizzle. I was very tired and dozed off on the bench on the right side. Willie, the movie technician, was sitting on the film boxes, and an Air Force hitchhiker was sitting on the opposite bench. The truck was enclosed in a plywood frame.

Vaguely I remember Willie singing "Don't fence me in", then I had a funny sensation. The road noise had stopped. Suddenly I knew that we had failed to make a curve on the wet pavement. Then the truck hit something, bounced up, and kept turning over, and over and over. I kept bouncing between the floor and the ceiling when I was finally thrown clear. I saw the truck, upside down. Somebody was screaming, "my God, please help me." The Air Force guy was covered in blood but seemed to be otherwise unhurt. "Get on the highway and stop first car and tell the driver to take you to the nearest Army Base."

My legs hurt terribly but I managed to struggle over the steep bank. I stopped the German car and told the driver that I was looking for an Army base. He drove me about two miles down the road to a Quartermaster Company. I told the guard that an American truck was wrecked and some people were trapped underneath. Within minutes, three trucks full of GI's were speeding toward the scene of the accident. They lifted the truck manually and freed the bodies beneath. The driver and Willie were unconscious; the man who was sitting in the passenger seat was seriously injured. As for myself and the Air Force guy we seemed to be unhurt except for the pain in our legs. Nevertheless, we were taken to the Hospital in Frankfurt for observation. Soon thereafter, Lieutenant Swann came and asked me to identify the bodies, Willy and the driver were dead.

We returned to Fulda, and it was a long time before I was able to forget this nightmare. I don't think that I will never hear the song, "Don't fence me in," without being reminded of that terrible ride from Frankfurt. Then some weeks later, I received notice to report to the Immigration Center in Frankfurt. Then three more weeks and I was transferred to a camp in Bremen. There I awaited the ship that would take me to the United States. I went about the town; Bremen was destroyed. I wondered if these people would ever forget what war really means and how much misery it had caused.

Finally, September 7, 1946 we were told that the ship would be leaving that night at 7:30pm. The ride to Bremerhaven was made by train. We were all happy, all of us on our way to the promised land, a boatload of approximately eight hundred refugees. As I approached the gangplank I looked for the name of the ship - SS Marine Marlin, a merchant marine ship, liberty class. I liked the sound of it. I went quickly to my assigned hammock, deposited my suitcase and returned to the deck to watch the crew cast off. The fog horn sounded, the lines were cast, and we were off.

I looked toward the mainland. Oh, the misery and the suffering I was leaving behind. I was sick of Europe. I lost faith that things would ever return to normal there. There would always be someone willing to swallow somebody else, and war will return once again. I wanted no more wars. I had my share. I wanted to get away from there, never to return. I wanted to live in peace. I wanted to have future worth living for, not a life of fear that my future would be denied me because I belonged to a minority group.

The sun was setting in the west and I felt that a chapter of my life was coming to an end. I had no regrets about leaving. I was confident that the new day would bring a new life in a land that would offer opportunities worth living for and fighting for.

I was happy.

THE END

Made in the USA
Lexington, KY
21 May 2017